Giovanni Andreozzi

True Stories & Other Works of Fiction

GIOVANNI ANDREAZZI

authorHOUSE®

AuthorHouse™
1663 Liberty Drive
Bloomington, IN 47403
www.authorhouse.com
Phone: 1-800-839-8640

First published by AuthorHouse 1/26/2010

ISBN: 978-1-4490-7458-6 (sc)

Printed in the United States of America
Bloomington, Indiana

This book is printed on acid-free paper.

Acknowledgements

The images for this book were done by Mela Saylor, the president of the Greater Canton Writer's Guild. When I first saw her drawings, ones that she had done for one of our Guild pamphlets, I was amazed. Here was an artist who drew like I thought. I asked her if she would be interested in doing the cover and some of the internal drawings to help spice up my book. She was delighted.

All I had to do was give her an idea for the front cover and a description of the various sections of the book. The sketches she showed me were phenomenal. It was as if she had performed a Vulcan Mind Meld and taken thoughts directly from me and put them on paper. Her drawings may be the best part of this, my sixth attempt at writing.

Again, I'd like to thank my editor, Bobbi-Lou, who was a character in my second novel, *Moonbeam*. She plodded through my drafts, patiently helping me to get my tenses and other grammatical errors corrected. I've made changes since her corrections were made, so any errors remaining are most likely mine.

Finally, I want to thank my family, some of whom are depicted in the family section and poetry. There were others who inspired me to write some of the stories and poetry, but are too numerous to mention.

True Stories and Other Works of Fiction is like my fourth book *Fairy Tales and Sea Stories*, the two mean about the same thing. Let me explain.

A fairy tale is made up, a sea story is an embellished version of fact with some untruths added in. Therefore, the listener cannot determine much difference between the fairy tale and the sea story.

Even though someone tries to write a "true story," it can't be exactly as it happened. I read somewhere that "you must question that which you hear, you should question that which you read, and question that which you see." So, when somebody writes non-fiction, it can't be exactly as it happened. By human nature, we interject some personal or other accounting of what we saw, heard, or felt. Two people at the same event will tell different versions of what they remember happening.

Some of the stories included in this collection are based on fact, but since I am relating them to you, I can't help but interject the stories with my own versions of what happened. In addition, I try to write an entertaining story. A story completely factual, were that possible, would probably be boring. Therefore, I titled this, my sixth book, as I view life – part true, part fiction.

PART ONE

My Family

The Scent Of A Limburger

**(Get it? Huh? Huh? Get it? Scent of a woman.
Scent of a limburger. Get it? Huh? Huh? Get it? Well, maybe not.)**

Our house was constructed just before WW II. The ten-foot long and six-foot wide kitchen only had room for one cook at a time. With the cabinets, sink, and stove on one side and the chimney enclosure, refrigerator, pantry, and stair access to the basement on the other, there was only a narrow, three-foot wide aisle in which to prepare meals. To the right of the stove was the living room and at the opposite end, was what we called a breakfast nook. Dad and Grandpa doubled the ten by ten-foot nook by expanding it out to meet the side of the new garage they had also built. Our ten-foot wide twenty-foot long breakfast nook was where Mom, Dad, my three sisters, and I ate all of our meals and where guests were entertained. In the late forties, the attached garage was a luxury that none of our neighbors enjoyed.

Dad wasn't too handy in the kitchen, and other than bacon and eggs on Sunday morning, he pretty much left all the cooking to Mom. So, whenever he did grab a cooking utensil other than a frying pan, or on a day other than Sunday, it got my sisters' and my attention.

One of those times he grabbed a skillet on a Saturday. Mom was across the street visiting with my grandma and Dad was hungry after coming home from a rare, Saturday work day. It was mid-afternoon when he walked in the door and noticed Mom was not home yet, so he headed to the refrigerator to see what he could find.

He liked limburger cheese. This odiferous food comes from Belgium and is named for the town of Limburg. It is one of those cheeses that must have been fed to prisoners during some ancient war until the jailers found that the cheese they were about to throw away but gave to their prisoners instead, didn't taste all that bad, especially if you had a cold and couldn't smell the odor of stinky feet that emanated from it.

It is a fermented cheese, probably from milk left to sour after absorbing brevibacterium linens, which is the same bacterium found on human skin. This is the same organism responsible for human body odor, hence its olfactory comparison to toe jam.

There was my father with a chunk of limburger cheese and two slices of bread. When he grabbed the frying pan we got really curious.

We could smell the cheese even as he sliced through it. He sandwiched it between the two slices of buttered-on-one-side rye bread and then into the frying pan. Placing the pan on the stove he lit the burner with a Blue-Tip kitchen match. That was when the fun started.

The smell was horrendous as the cheese melted and ran out of the bread and into the hot pan to bubble up like a yellow and gold Mount Vesuvius. As the odor reached its peak, like a hundred dirty socks tromping through the kitchen, Mom walked through the door.

I rarely saw her get excited, but she did this time as the stench hit her full in the face. Since it was a winter day and well below freezing, she was reluctant to open a window, but she did anyway. The kitchen window flew open, the front and back doors were slammed open, and Dad headed to the back porch to devour his sandwich.

"Take the pan with you and bury it in the backyard," she said.

My sisters and I headed to the attic to avoid some of her fury. The next day, out of curiosity, I looked for the cheese. The lingering smell dwelt in the house for days, but the cheese was gone, as was the frying pan which I never saw again.

A Horseradish Of A Different Color

**(Get it? Huh? Huh? Get it? Horse of a different color.
Horseradish of a different color. Get it? Huh? Huh? Get it?)**

Our basement was the largest room in our little ranch house. It was unfinished when I was a kid, but it did have a linoleum floor. The closed-in coal bin, a large coal-fired furnace, and a fruit cellar took up about half of the basement to the left of the descending stairs. Starting in the middle and lined up against the bare, concrete-block walls on the opposite side of the stairs, was a double steel laundry tub, the washing machine (an old one with the wringer rollers on top for squeezing the clothes semi-dry), and next to the washing machine rested an old-fashioned, white-porcelain and cast-iron gas stove where Mom did her canning and jelly making. The floor sloped to a floor drain just under the double sinks. Occasionally, during heavy rains, the basement would flood and water would pour into the drain from three sides of the basement. A clothes line was strung lengthwise from one side of the wall to the other where Mom hung the laundry in the winter and on those rainy-day Mondays.

When the weather was not conducive to playing outside, my mom had not hung up clothes to dry, and the basement was not a river, my sisters and I would ride tricycles, play hopscotch, and otherwise entertain ourselves in open space of the forty-by-forty-foot room.

Dad loved horseradish. He would put it on everything, including toasted limburger cheese sandwiches and then complain that it wasn't fresh enough. He liked it freshly ground, right from the radish to his plate, so it was not unusual for him to want to make his own.

A man whom he worked with grew the radish and gave Dad some. Coming home from work that September afternoon, he walked through the door with a box of long, white tubers of the swollen root from the horseradish plant. Its botanical name is *Armoracia rusticana*, and it is a perennial plant of the Brassicaceae family which includes mustard and cabbages. The plant is probably native to southeastern Europe and western Asia, but is popular around the world today. It grows up to five feet tall and is mainly cultivated for its large white, tapered root.

The horseradish root itself has hardly any aroma. When cut or grated, however, enzymes from the damaged plant cells break down sinigrin (a glucosinolate) to produce allyl isothiocyanate (mustard oil), which irritates the sinuses and eyes similarly to the mustard gas used by the Germans in World War I. Someone poisoned by mustard gas would take three to four weeks, to die. Once grated, if not used immediately or mixed in vinegar, the root darkens and loses its pungency and becomes unpleasantly bitter when exposed to air and heat. That was what Dad complained about with the horseradish he got from the neighborhood grocery store.

"It's rancid," he would declare. "Look at the color! It's brown, not white like horseradish should be."

"Take that into the basement," Mom said without hesitating after she saw him with his box of roots. The toasted-limburger-cheese-sandwich smell was still lingering in the sense organs of her mind. Dad obediently took his prize down the stairs.

The next morning was a Saturday and Dad didn't have to go to work, nor did he have chores to do around the house. He was free to do what he wanted which was to make the freshest horseradish known to modern man. He gathered up the hand-operated meat grinder from the kitchen pantry, the one Mom used to make ground meat for her much coveted, home-made meatballs, and headed for the basement with a bottle of vinegar. He kept empty canning jars in the basement as almost everyone did years ago. The jars were used to can everything from tomatoes to jelly. Back when I was a kid, people did a lot more of their own food processing until supermarkets made such mundane necessities a thing of the past.

I heard him clanging and clinking around getting things ready and I knew enough not to bother him when he was being creative. My curiosity overcame me when he started talking to himself.

"All set to make the best horseradish in the world," I overheard him say.

I crept slowly down the stairs and was surprised when he beckoned me over to the large, double laundry tub next to the washing machine.

I was surprised when, in a jovial mood, he apparently was going to let me help.

"Come on Son," he said, smiling. "You can help feed the grinder."

I bounded over to where he was and he handed me one of the tubers, which didn't at all smell like what he spread on just about everything he ate. But when I shoved the first of the roots into the grinder, it was a different story. I didn't stay long.

With both hands on the handle of the grinder's crank he turned the little gear box activating the screw-like shaft that mashed and shoved the root toward the shredder at the end of the grinder. What came out and fell into the pan waiting in the bottom of the tub was definitely freshly ground horseradish.

"Now that's the color horseradish should be," he said with pride. Holding the pan up to his nose, he took a deep breath and as he held it up to me, I did the same.

After what could only be described as inhaling a forest full of pine needles, my eyes burst forth a flood of water and my head recoiled. I looked at my father with tears in my eyes and saw that he was not immune from the acrid smell either.

"You can go, Son," he said, sounding like a man with a noose around his neck falling halfway through the trap door.

I bolted up the stairs holding my breath the entire way. When I reached the kitchen at the top of the stairs and took a deep breath, I recoiled again. The smell was everywhere. It far surpassed burning limburger cheese in intensity. Dad, however, was not to be dismayed. I heard him grinding and choking away in the basement.

My sisters came running down the stairs crying and coughing. Mom was in the backyard hanging up clothes on the hand-operated clothes dryer, but a cloud of vapor reached her that must have been similar to those mustard gas attacks.

In one giant step, she made it to the back door and slammed the door shut. She then leapt the two stairs into the kitchen and shut the door to the basement, thus isolating Dad and his prize condiment in a sealed forty-by-forty foot hole in the ground.

When Dad had four quart-sized mason jars filled and sealed, he emerged from the basement with Godzilla-red eyes and reeking of horseradish, but he also had a triumphant smile on his face. As neighbors walked in front of our house on their evening stroll, they pulled handkerchiefs out of their pockets to cover their noses and crossed to the other side of the street. I just went to my room to read comic books while I waited out the three weeks to die.

Thank God, the smell of freshly-ground horseradish didn't linger for days as the toasted-limburger had, but gradually dissipated through the open windows on that mild, fall evening.

Straightening Nails

As a young boy growing up in the 50's I always wanted to help Dad. He always had to work two jobs to keep us housed, clothed, and fed, and he had both a day job and a night job. The day job was as a draftsman and stone carver at a monument shop, which must have not paid a whole lot. His second jobs were: meat inspector, bakery truck driver, rose bush pruner, and when he got a portable sandblaster and air compressor, he would go to the cemeteries in surrounding counties and cut the last two numbers of the death date on monuments.

So, when he had work to do around the house, I was eager to pitch in and spend what could have been quality time with Dad. Other kid's Dads took them to the lake to fish, to ballgames, or to other father-son outings. Working two jobs left Dad precious little time to do what needed to be done to maintain our house.

Most of his do-it-yourself projects began with left-over crate material from his primary job. Polished and finished granite stones were shipped to the monument shop from Barre, Vermont encased in protective wooden crates. The wood which was not shipped back for reuse ended up at our house for various projects such as concrete form work, shelving, or outdoor furniture, and I wanted to help Dad.

"Sure, Son," he would say. "You can help me. Here's a hammer."

Oh boy! I thought. *A hammer*! *I'm really going to be able to help Dad.*

I stood by eagerly, hammer in hand, awaiting his first command. Was he going to have me build a table, install some shelves in the garage, make a box to store tools? What will be my first job? I watched wide eyed as he skillfully wielded a small pry bar and yanked out the nails from the ends of the wood boards that had originally held the crates together. When he was done with the first pile of boards, he looked at me with a smile.

"While I work on those other boards, pick up the nails I just pulled and straighten them out like this." He then demonstrated the art of holding a large deformed ten-penny spike against the concrete floor of the garage. With the bend pointing up, he then taped on the bend of the nail until it was as close to straight as could be attained. "Now you try it."

I did, and with a little additional instruction, I got the nail almost to its original shape.

"Good job, Son," he said, as he held the nail up for inspection. "When you're done just put them in the coffee cans, big nails in one can and small in the other." That said, he tossed the spike in the closest can with a resounding clang and went back to pulling more nails from the pile of wood.

I gathered up the nails from the garage floor being careful not to disturb his nail pulling. I took my hammer and carefully placed each nail with the high side up and tapped it back so that it was straight. I was very meticulous with each of the nails, treating them like they were the most precious of rare metals. I examined each one carefully as if I were selecting the choicest cuts of beef from the grocery store.

He finished pulling nails from the stack of wood and took the boards down to the basement to measure, cut, and assemble them for the latest project. After I had straightened all the nails, I went outside to play with my sisters.

After Dad died, my sisters and I had the job of clearing all the accumulated stuff in the house we had grown up in. We had a large dumpster parked in the driveway and filled it up with broken lawn mowers, non-working weed eaters, large electric motors, and other items we could not take to Goodwill.

In the garage, on a shelf, I found an assortment of coffee cans. Opening the lids I found what must have been every nail I had ever straightened, unused and rusty. It was then that I realized that what I thought was help, was just a ploy to keep me busy and out of his way – make work. I guessed that all boys back in the 50's must have been expert nail straighteners, at least the ones who wanted to help Dad.

S.O.S.

I don't know if the Navy still serves for breakfast a particular delicacy nicknamed, affectionately, SOS. The first time I had it in boot camp in 1962, I thought it was great. That was my first breakfast away from home when my family wasn't with me, and it was new food to me. I was hungry, too, having been awakened at 4:30, the same way as every morning in boot camp, to the clanging of the drill instructor's, baton inside an empty metal trash can. After we got cleaned up and put on the same clothes we had to wear until we were issued our uniforms, we were marched in darkness to the chow hall at the Great Lakes Naval Training Center in Illinois. The day before I had traveled by train from my home town and didn't remember eating a whole lot.

The official name of SOS, I believe, is chipped beef on toast. The unofficial name stood for "something" on a shingle. Only the "something" was a four letter word which I'm sure you can guess. Dried beef, suspended in a white, thickened sauce of butter, milk, and flour (the something) was slopped onto toast (the shingle) in the large section of the metal dining tray as I walked blurry eyed along the serving line. The entrée met the three requisites for feeding hungry recruits who had a day of physical activity ahead of them: it was easy to make, filling, and quickly consumed. I have to admit, it tasted pretty good and it was something I had never had before.

The next morning, we were awakened the same way with the baton in the trash can which was also affectionately called the "something" can. "Something" was a favorite word that described a lot of military life. One of the first insults that I had learned in the Navy was, "she was so ugly, she had a face like a bent "something" can."

That second morning, we did our three "s's," (something, shower, and shave) and then hungrily marched off to the chow hall. Standing silently in line—no talking was allowed—I anticipated my second breakfast in boot camp. I held my tray in front of the first server and he slapped down two pieces of toast. The second server dumped a ladle of SOS on top of that. Okay, I liked the stuff, it tasted fine, and it had the necessary calories to get me through the busy morning, so I "chowed" down.

The third breakfast was not SOS, but the fourth was. We weren't supposed to talk but, when the drill instructor was at the far side of the room, I whispered to the man next to me.

"What's this stuff called?"

"SOS," he whispered back.

"What's that mean?" I said back.

"'Something' on a shingle," he said.

So I picked up a little military jargon. After about the tenth serving, I started to play with the little pieces of dried reddish-brown beef, as if I were looking under each one for a prize. I re-named it "same-old-'something'," and by the time I got out of boot camp, I never wanted to see it again.

It was my first full day at home on leave from boot camp. My parents were proud of me, my oldest sister was about to get married while I was still home, and this was my first breakfast in three months with my family. It was a Saturday and usually Dad did the cooking, but today, my newly-to-be-wed sister, in anticipation of feeding her soon-to-be husband, was trying out her cooking skills for just me and Dad. My youngest sister and Mom were still in bed, and my middle sister was away in nursing school.

The night before, as a rite of passage, even though I was underage, Dad drank a shot and a beer with me while we compared horror stories of boot camps, his being twenty years before, but the scenario had not changed much over the years. I felt like he had finally accepted me as man and the feeling was good. At the breakfast table, while my sister worked away in the kitchen, Dad and I continued discussing the navy, where I would be going on my first duty assignment, and what I would be doing after that.

"Breakfast is ready," she said proudly as she brought two plates of food to the table.

Her feelings were immediately damaged as Dad and I looked at what she had slaved over at a hot stove and both laughed as if on cue. It was, SOS!

My sister was nearly in tears before we explained why we both had the same reaction to her hard morning's labor. I hadn't mentioned the SOS to Dad the night before, but he knew by my disgusted expression upon seeing the plate of food, that the navy had not changed in those twenty years. My sister forgave us after hearing the explanation and we ate what she had prepared.

It was good.

Gnocchi Savvy

(And the Brother-in-law to be)

When a daughter in an Italian family brings home a potential suitor to meet the relatives, it's an important event. My next to oldest sister had recently met a man she thought was "Mr. Right." It was the second Mr. Right, the first having died a year or so earlier after a long fight with muscular dystrophy. Since this was her second potential husband, it was not as big an event as her first, but the family-meal, meet-the-suitor tradition was still the same.

His name is John, my name is John, and my father's name was John. This could have been confusing if I had not been called Johnny and my father was simply known as Dad. At least it was not confusing at family gatherings, but when all three of us were around other people, an exclamation of "hey, John!" would have received three "whats" in return, and often it did.

The meet-the-suitor meal had to be prepared at home, and it had to be traditional Italian fare. Nothing could be more Italian than gnocchi. I've been told the word means "potato pillow" in Italian and they resemble little pillows, at least the way they were made in the northern part of Italy from where my family immigrated. My family's pronunciation of the word was nyaw-key, but most Americans pronounce it no-key or knock-key as getting the nyaw sound right is not easy. Gnocchi are made with potatoes, eggs, semolina or regular flour, salt and pepper. They were one of Dad's, and the rest of the family's favorite Italian dishes.

Gnocchi had to be cooked the same day in which they were made. The flour, eggs, cooked riced potatoes, and seasonings were mixed in a large bowl until the consistency was achieved that only an Italian mother or grandmother knew was correct. The dough was then rolled into long ropes on a floured surface, usually a wooden gnocchi board, and then cut into one-inch cubes. If left too long after they were cut, they would tend to pull themselves together, using little gnocchi gravitational force fields, and reform into one big ball of dough again. So as soon as they were prepared – some Italians used a fork to make an indentation on one side of the pillow, but my family never did – they were shoved into a large pot of boiling, salted water. They were so heavy that they sank like rocks tossed into a pond. It was important to have lots of water and a slotted spoon for retrieving the gnocchi when done.

In about ten minutes, the pillows reappeared, floating to the surface. When they floated, they were light and soft and ready for the sauce. Using the slotted spoon, they were retrieved, drained, and placed in a bowl. Red spaghetti sauce was added, and sometimes a little Italian parsley or basil leaves to give the dish the red, white, and green colors of the Italian flag. I don't know which came first, the flag or gnocchi, but since a lot of Italian dishes have white pasta, red sauce, and a green garnish, either parsley or basil, I'll bet the food came before the flag and the flag copied from it. Occasionally butter would be melted over the gnocchi instead of the traditional red sauce.

They are delicious, but they also cause a serious thirst. On their own, the little pillows have a tendency to absorb water much like the sodium polyacrylate crystals in disposable diapers. Of course there is a lot of garlic in the sauce along with a fair helping of salt. Drinking liquids to quench the thirst causes the gnocchi to swell and distend the stomach. As kids, we learned not to eat so many, but unsuspecting guests had no idea what they were to experience.

I was home with my wife for the first time since we had been married, my younger sister and her husband were there, and my parents. I had never met my sister's suitor, and the first thing I noticed when she brought him home, was that he was a big man. He was not only six-feet, three inches tall, but broad in the shoulders. I had heard that he was an ex-FBI agent and highway patrolman and those two organizations don't usually hire wimps.

He also had a big-man's appetite. We never thought to warn him of gnocchi's hydrophilic, or affinity for water, characteristic. When we sat down to eat, we passed our plates to my mother as we always did and she determined how much would be apportioned to each person. That tradition may have come from the old country when there really wasn't enough food to fill everyone's plate and the mother knew how much was available. Ensuring that those who needed more food to sustain energy to provide for the wellbeing of the family was a necessity. Therefore, the mother filled the plates. We always had more than enough food, and the little pillows always had a way of disappearing no matter how many were in the bowl.

Gnocchi was a meal in itself and meat was rarely served with it. A salad before the gnocchi was in order, Garlic bread, and of course a little red wine were the only other food items on the table.

My mother doled out a generous portion to our guest and passed it back to him. The entire time he ate, he proclaimed how good they were. He passed his plate for seconds and then thirds. Nothing makes an Italian mother happier than a person with a healthy appetite, so she filled his plate with each helping. Except for my father who displayed no emotion, the rest of us sitting around the table were amazed at how much he packed away. My mother was pleased as much as we were amazed. My father's idea of a family meal was no talking, only eating. While the rest of us were talking and asking the guest questions to find out more about him, my father just ate in silence.

The meal ended with coffee and pizzelles for dessert. Pizzelles are a lacy cookie made from eggs, flour, and sugar. Extracts such as anise, vanilla, or almond are added for flavoring. The dough is poured into a pizzelle maker that looks like a small waffle iron. A minute or two later, the wafer thin cookie with geometric impressions and browned on both sides is ready to cool. The light cookie is a nice compliment to the heaviness of the gnocchi.

After the dishes were done, everyone but my parents went to the church auditorium to play volleyball with some friends. After the first set, the suitor headed to the water cooler for a drink. The gnocchi were exerting their affinity for water and together with the exercise, he was getting thirstier by the minute. I looked at my sister and smiled, but she didn't say anything to him. After all, he was an adult and what could we have told him, "don't drink?"

Drinking water was necessary, for without the water the gnocchi would have sucked the moisture from all his internal organs and he would dry up like a worm on a hot sidewalk after a summer's rain. By the fifth set, and many trips to the water fountain, he was in obvious pain. For one thing, he couldn't jump anymore and was slowed down by his swelling gut. By the end of the game, he was lying on the floor of the elevated stage, belt buckle loosened, and the top part of his pants undone. His stomach was now distended as if he had swallowed the volleyball we had been playing with. He started to moan, a long, low rumbling groan like that which comes from deep in the earth when a volcano is about to erupt. Nothing from his FBI or trouper training had prepared him for this.

"What's happening," he asked, but instead of sympathy, he only received laughs from my sisters and me. We related to the other players what had happened and then we all had a good laugh at his expense as he lay suffering on the stage, waiting to die. As we helped him to the car, we explained the art of just eating a few gnocchi, so as not to suffer later. The next day, other than stretch marks across his stomach as if he had given birth to full term quintuplets, he was okay, but much more gnocchi savvy.

The Cana

Not that I didn't deserve it, but my mother did break my wristwatch with the cana (káh-nah). I don't remember if this was before or after she had broken a plate over my head, but it doesn't really matter.

The cana is a hardwood paddle used primarily for stirring polenta, an Italian peasant dish consisting of water and corn meal. Some might call it mush. To an Italian, it was a staple, and when mixed with cheese or hard salami, is delicious. The cana, Italian for cane, is about eighteen inches long, the top half being round and the bottom half flattened and about two inches wide enabling it to be moved somewhat easily through the thick polenta.

The secondary use for the cana is to threaten and sometimes inflict corporal punishment. Having a narrow business end, it moves easily through the air striking its target with a loud smack. Unless something like a wristwatch gets in the way.

"You want me to get the cana?" was an often heard phrase when I was around.

Nothing more needed to be said, since I could remember the first time when I didn't heed the warning. There had been no threat the time Mom broke my watch. The cana happened to be already deployed and ready for action.

When it had happened, the busting of the plate over the back of my head was a surprise to me. I didn't even get the usual warning. All I heard before I felt the whack and the descending shards of glass was "I could just...I could just" and then a brief flash of light. I don't remember what I had done to deserve it, but I know Mom hardly ever acted in anger.

She usually just said, "Wait 'til your father gets home."

His favorite choice of weapons was his belt, with me over his knee. More than once I got even, sort of, by letting my bladder go on his thigh.

This ended the thrashing more than "Daddy, please stop," or "I won't do it again," uttered between sobs or yells of pain. He somehow was aware that I would "do it again" and I didn't disappoint very often.

Relating this "remember when" story after Mom had died, my sisters told me that the plate was already cracked and Mom was just taking it to the garage to throw it away. Sitting at the kitchen table with my back towards her, between the kitchen and the trash can in the garage, I had presented an easy target. It was just a matter of her remembering something that I had recently done and then the "I could just…I could just."

Pa-ping! A broken plate.

A little older, taller, and with my watch on my arm, I had done something else to anger Mom. Whatever I had done, doing it when Mom had the cana in her hand was not the smartest move I had ever made. There was no "I could just…I could just" or "you want me to get the cana?"

When she raised her arm, cana at the ready, I instinctively put my hand up to block the blow. Because I was taller than Mom, when it came down, it hit me straight on the wrist and I heard the crunch of cana against crystal. I don't remember any pain, but I did yell out, "My watch! My watch!"

Not long after that I went in the Navy and was never blessed with the cana again.

The Father-In-Law and the Bottle of Gin
Or
We didn't know the casket was Hollow!

I loved my in-laws. That sounds strange, but I did, almost as much as my own parents. My wife for 32 years and I, because we lived away from Ohio most of our lives, did not get to see them very often. When we did, it was always enjoyable. We spent almost the entire visit around the kitchen table, eating, talking, or playing scrabble. There was always an ample supply of beer and gin, and my father-in-law loved his gin.

They spent the last years of their lives in a small house on the side of a hill overlooking the Scioto River in Portsmouth, Ohio. Through two large picture windows, the view over the valley to the west was fantastic. The only downside was the steep road and driveway to get to the house, but they didn't go out much after they retired.

I can remember a game of scrabble with my wife and mother-in-law where I tried to attach the word "so" to the end of a word with an s in it. My intent was to pluralize the word "so," but my mother-in-law would have none of it. Then I tried to say that it was the distress signal, SOS.

"No abbreviations or proper nouns," she said.

"If it isn't in the dictionary, it can't be used," she added, holding up the dictionary she kept on the table for each game.

Other words that I had tried to use that were in my much larger dictionary were not allowed either as they were not in her thirty-year-old Webster. No argument, no points, remove the tiles, and forfeit your turn.

The rest of the visit and subsequent visits I was referred to as the son-in-law who tried to use "sos" in a game of scrabble. I didn't mind the good-natured ribbing, in fact I kind of looked forward to it.

We got the bad news one day that my father-in-law had prostate cancer. Doctors were able to remove most of it, but it had metastasized and a tumor started to grow in his brain. He had surgery to remove that too, but that type of cancer is almost always fatal. We decided to pay them a visit since it might be our last chance to see him alive. Other than the scars from surgery and some other after effects of chemotherapy, he was quite fine, but we all knew it was a losing battle.

It wasn't long before he succumbed to the cancer and we returned to Southern Ohio for the funeral. As one of the males in the family, I was to be a pallbearer.

The night before the funeral, most of the entire family (he had two sons and three daughters from his first marriage and three daughters from his second) were gathered in the small house on the hill. We were all talking, eating the food that friends and neighbors had brought, and drinking beer when the younger son started bragging about his taste in beer.

He was, he thought, a connoisseur of fine beer and would only drink one or two certain brands as the other beers "tasted terrible." As he displayed one of the bottles that he had brought, we could see that his brand came in bottles with twist-off caps and was expensive. What the rest of us drank came in cans and was cheap. He proudly passed around his beer to allow us to "taste the difference for ourselves." Frankly, it was good, but not worth the three to four times the price of good ol' Schlitz, Bud, or whatever the store had on sale, and I told him so. That made him all the more snooty.

It was after he had left, that I decided to have some fun with him.

Having come the farthest and having gotten there first, my wife and I were staying at the house. When the others left for the night, I rummaged around in the trash and recovered two empty bottles of his beer and two twist-off caps. With my wife and mother-in-law as witnesses, I carefully, so as not to make it foam too much, poured cans of Budweiser into the empty bottles. I then capped them, marked them with a pen, and placed them in the refrigerator in the cardboard six pack holding his other, unaltered beers.

The next morning was calling hours and the funeral. It dawned a nice, sunny, cool day, and my wife and I drove with my mother-in-law to the funeral.

During the family-only visiting hours, my wife and I approached the casket by ourselves. Aware that he liked his gin, we were going to send him on his way with his favorite alcoholic beverage.

We had purchased a one-serving, airplane sized, glass bottle of Gilbey's, his favorite brand of gin. Thinking that the others, especially my mother-in-law, would disapprove of what we were about to do we kept our plan to ourselves. Unaware that the wife was supposed to visit the casket first, we went to the casket before any of the others. Luckily, no one noticed or said anything. With Sally blocking the view from the others, I pulled the little bottle out of my pocket, reached in, and shoved it down the side of the casket and out of view.

Plunk, we both heard. The bottle had fallen to the bottom of the metal casket, but no one else appeared to have heard it. No one had told us that the casket was hollow under the body.

We looked at each other in a panic, but didn't say anything. Quietly we went to the back of the viewing area. All throughout the calling hours we discussed what would happen when the casket was carried to the hearse, and from there into the church, all the way up the aisle of the church back to the hearse, and from the hearse to the gravesite. Would the bottle roll around and clunk against the sides of the casket while everyone was silently grieving and wondering what was that God-awful noise coming from the bottom of the casket?

We didn't know the casket was hollow!

When he was alone, we approached the funeral director and told him what had happened.

"Why didn't you give it to me," he said. "I would have put it in one of his suit pockets."

We didn't know the casket was hollow!

"Don't worry," he added. "At the end of the service while everyone is waiting by the hearse and before we call in the pallbearers, we will remove the body, retrieve the bottle, and place it in a suit coat pocket." He had a why-didn't-you-give-it-to-me-first look on his face.

Soon it was time to go to the church for the service. We were all ushered into the waiting area until the casket was made ready to transport. We waited, and waited, and waited. People were getting restless.

"What's taking so long?" several asked.

Sally and I knew what was taking so long. We didn't know the casket was hollow!

What seemed like hours had passed, but finally the funeral director beckoned the pallbearers in with a glance toward Sally and I with a look of reassurance. He still had the why-didn't-you-give-it-to-me-first look on his face. By now, I had decided correcting our mistake was all part of his job and felt no guilt whatsoever. I was more relieved that the bottle of gin would not rattle around in the casket like a ball bearing in a metal bucket, especially while I was helping to carry it.

Without a rattle we carried the casket to the hearse and from the hearse to the front of the church. It was heavy and I had a hard time going up and down the stairs to the church. I was wondering if the others were carrying the same load, and what would have happened had there been rattling noises coming from the casket. Would I have been able to contain any laughter welling up from my throat? I was thankful I didn't have to answer that question.

When the funeral procession turned the last corner to the cemetery, just outside the gates was a fire truck with a dozen firemen standing at attention and saluting. My father-in-law had been a retired fire chief and their respects were being paid. I choked back some tears as we passed by on the way into the cemetery. Had we thought of it, we could have had the casket carried to the cemetery on the back of a fire truck with the firemen as pallbearers.

As it was, it was a teary ceremony at the burial site, but soon it was over and we headed back to the house on the hill for our last get together.

Relieved that the funeral was over and Bob was in his final resting place, we were able to relax a little. We ate some more of the food left over from the night before and had started to drink beer. I offered to get a beer for my snooty brother-in-law.

"Make sure that it's one of mine and not that rot gut you guys drink," he said.

"Of course," I responded.

I went to the refrigerator and pulled out a six pack of my "rot gut" beers for me and the others who drank rot gut. Making sure I had a marked bottle, I grabbed one of the beers that I had prepared the night before. Double checking it to make sure that it was one of the "stealth buds," I handed it to him. He twisted off the cap and took a drink right from the bottle.

"Ah," he said. "Now this is a beer to be proud of."

My wife and mother-in-law shot a glance my way and I just smiled back at them and gave a little nod to confirm what they already knew. We discussed the events of the day and Sally and I related the story about the little bottle of gin with our excuse that "we didn't know the casket was hollow!"

Everyone thought that we did the right thing by telling the funeral director. By the time the story was over, I noticed that snooty had finished his beer.

"Let me get you another," I said as I finished the last of mine, got up, and headed for the refrigerator."

"Thanks," snooty said.

When I got back to the table, I handed him the second disguised Bud and, trying to imitate the old beer commercial, intoned, "This Bud's for you."

"What?" he asked, dumbfoundedly, twisting the cap off the bottle.

"I said, this Bud's for you," I repeated as I sat down and popped the top on my can of Bud.

"What does that mean?" he asked, taking a drink from the bottle.

"The last beer that you had and that one, are good ol' rot gut Budweiser." I said with a smirk.

"No it's not!" he said.

"Ask your mother and sister," I said, without diverting my gaze.

He looked toward both of them, and without saying anything, they both nodded yes. His mouth dropped open.

"Just to prove that you couldn't tell the difference between the expensive beer and my cheap rot gut, after you left last night I fished two of your empty bottles from the trash. I poured Bud in them, replaced the caps, and put them in the fridge."

He did not respond, but got up, took the beer to the sink, and poured it down the drain.

"Let's go," he said to his companion.

Leaving his remaining beers in the frig, he walked out the door, got in his car and left.

After Bob's funeral, the family reunions stopped and I never saw ol' snooty again. The day I had played the prank, I couldn't help but think that Bob was in heaven, enjoying the bottle of gin we had sent with him, and snickering along with us.

PART TWO

Scary Stuff

TELL-A-TALE HEART

Chapter One

It was a dark and stormy night...

Well, maybe not, but that's the way Charles Schulz's Snoopy would start a story (Edward Bulwer-Lytton actually was the first to use that incipit in the novel, *Paul Clifford*).

The illustration she had done for him took her four days to complete. She had worked extremely hard on it, a drawing of a broken heart, because, after all, he was a first-rate, well-known writer. Getting one of her works on the front cover of one of his books would be a godsend and the recognition inside the book could boost her sales more than ten-fold.

But he turned out to be a first-rate, unknown bastard and decided to do something different not using her artwork. They had had a "gentlemen's agreement" on the price, so when he brushed her off with an e-mail, not even so much as a thank you, or even a phone call for that matter, she was angry.

She had delayed her trip to Taos so she could finish her broken heart drawing, a wasted effort to say the least. When she stormed out of her Denver studio, the floor was still littered with the first sketches she had tossed out, thinking them "not worthy of his book." Taking the broken heart drawing with her, she stepped over the scattered sketches, leaving them until she returned. Then she planned to have a ceremonial burning where her anger would go up and away from her with the smoke the fire would create.

On her first day, while setting up the paintings at her Gallery in the square at Taos, a Native American family stopped to admire her paintings. It seemed the old man who was with them had taken a fancy to one drawing in particular, one of the landscape west of Albuquerque.

It wasn't one of her best works and she was not really all that pleased with it, so it sat next to the "heart."

"How much is that painting?" the young girl asked her in a timid voice. "My grandfather said it reminds him of where he grew up as a little boy. We haven't much money, but he really likes it."

"Then please take it," she heard herself reply. "I will give it to you as a gift to my first customer of the day."

The little girl went back to her grandfather and said something to him in a language she had never heard before. She had traveled the world over and spoke in several languages, even Japanese, but never tried to learn the tongues of the people who were here in America first.

The little girl came back excitedly and said, "My grandfather is a medicine man and can pay your kindness with his skills. Is there anything he could do for you?"

"Yeah," she said without hesitation. "Put a curse on the painting next to the landscape he wants, the one of the broken heart."

That was the beginning of the nightmare!

...I told the little girl to put the curse on the painting as a joke, she thought, but the little girl did not smile. She only looked at the picture of the heart, walked up to the landscape painting and took it gently off the easel. She carried the painting back to her grandfather who was leaning on a gnarled cane that looked as if it were made from the branch of a mesquite tree. The little girl spoke to him again in that ancient language. He gave an understanding nod as he took the landscape and held it out to gaze upon it.

He stared at the painting as if he could see through it and into the past. As he handed the painting back to his granddaughter, a tear rolled down that ancient face and caressed a crease in his cheek before falling into the dust at his feet. He raised his eyes toward me and looked as though he were probing deep within my soul. I felt a tingle in my spine and the hair on my arms and the back of my neck stood straight out. He then turned his head slowly and fixed his gaze upon the heart. He strode deliberately over to the painting and when there, he rested his cane against the wall next to the front of the gallery. He reached deep inside the tattered denim jacket he wore and pulled a brown leather pouch from a pocket next to his own heart.

He placed one end of the pouch in his mouth and held onto it with only the gums that were left when teeth had eroded away from years of chewing peyote. With his right hand he pulled on the other side of the pouch opening it only far enough to reach in with the leathery fingers of his left hand. From the pouch emerged a small, bone-like object and once it was fully released from its leather home, it looked like the leg and claw of a bird. It could have been an eagle's judging by its size, but I could only guess what bird it had belonged to. He released the pouch from his mouth and reached out with the claw and seemed to stroke the picture, not quite touching it while he chanted in that tongue I could not understand. I imagined the old Indian as a child with a slingshot stalking birds to try his skill as a hunter, finally slaying one and bagging its claw, leg still attached, as a trophy.

I was mesmerized and did not know how long he stood there, claw in hand chanting, but eventually he returned the claw to the pouch and tucked it back beneath his jacket. He retrieved his cane, turned away from me, and headed to where his granddaughter was standing with the landscape drawing. The old medicine man never looked at me, not even a nod of gratitude. Evidently in his mind, the service he had performed was enough of a payment and no other acknowledgement was forthcoming. My eyes were fixed on his every movement as the two of them walked with the painting down the street, around the corner, and out of my life.

"Well, that was something," I muttered to myself. "What should I do now with this accursed painting?"

She didn't have time to dwell on what to do with the supposedly cursed painting too long since customers, tourists from the east she guessed, stopped to admire some of her other sidewalk displays. One of them started asking her questions and she was glad for the interruption of her thoughts about the broken heart painting.

At the end of the day, she put her paintings inside the gallery, the last being the heart, but instead of displaying it in the window with some of the others, she took it to the back of the gallery and laid it on the table. She would mail it tomorrow, she decided.

I'll send it to that asshole, she thought.

Chapter Two

She mailed the picture with a note which read:

Dear Author,

This is the painting I agreed to create for you for the cover of your latest novel. Since you have decided to use another design, I have no need for this one anymore, so it is yours to do with as you see fit.

She wanted to vent her anger at him with a nasty note, but decided that would just be a waste of energy. She had had a good showing in Taos and made enough on what she had sold to last her a few months. *I don't need his commission*, she thought. *I will get by just fine.*

His decision still hurt her deeply and the time spent on the painting was gone forever.

A month later she arrived home to find a message on her answering machine. It was him and he was frantic.

The picture had arrived at his house in Vermont. He didn't open it at first, but set it aside. Not because he wasn't curious about what was in the package, but because his heartburn was acting up. More precisely it was GERD. He had skipped his medicine that morning so he set the package aside and went to the kitchen to get an Omeprazole capsule. Only this time there wasn't the instant relief that he had felt in the past, so he sat in his recliner and eased it back as far as it would go. An hour later, the heartburn was worse, only now he felt dizzy when he tried to stand and there was some pain in his left shoulder.

I may be having a heart attack, he thought. So, he got in his car and headed down the mountain. He knew that if he was having a heart attack, he should not be driving, but by the time emergency vehicles could get to him as far up the side of the mountain as he lived, he could be dead anyway. To avoid any traffic, he took the back roads, all gravel, to within five minutes of the emergency room. Strangely enough, as soon as he got a mile or so down the road leading away from his house, the pain started to subside.

I better get to the hospital anyway, he thought. *Just in case.*

He arrived at the emergency room and was taken immediately to one of the rooms where tests were started and he received the attention of the entire medical staff. They all knew who he was, the famous author who lived up on Blueberry Hill. Any patient with a suspected heart attack would have received the same attention he received in this small hospital, but not as quickly or with as much concern.

"Just to be safe," Dr. Nosebomb said, "we'll keep you overnight for observation."

The next morning with all tests negative, he signed a release and left the hospital, but not before also signing several of his books the staff had brought to his room. He loved the attention his writings received. His only stop before heading back up the mountain was at the local Dunkin' Donuts to get a large coffee. There was a fog in the valley that morning, but the sun was above the gray mist and would burn through by ten or eleven o'clock. Halfway up the mountain he drove out of the foggy veil and into the bright sunshine with the fall foliage dazzlingly lining the country roads.

As soon as he got to his driveway, the pain started again. *Maybe it's the altitude or the changing weather*, he thought. *It is the autumn season and there was a full moon last night.*

When he got into his house, the pain became worse, especially when he passed the package in his studio. He picked up the package and a fiery pain shot up his left arm. He laid the package on the table in his office and ripped it open with his right hand.

"Shit!" he said when he recognized the picture and read the note. "That bitch is trying to make me feel guilty. Tonight I'll start a fire in the fireplace with this painting. Screw her!"

Chapter Three

His girlfriend, Ginny, came over to his house that evening for a romantic night – a candlelight dinner, a movie in front of a crackling fireplace, some snuggling on the couch, and then, who knows. Only it was going to be different, a lot different. The dinner went okay. The menu included cooked veal Florentine, some mashed, bourbon sweet potatoes, a side of his home-made pumpkin butter, steamed asparagus, and, of course, some wine. He picked out a bottle of his home-made merlot for the main course and, to serve with the poppy-seed kolaches he had made, Hogue Cellars, late-harvest Riesling.

She volunteered to clear the table while he lit the pile of wood in the fireplace that he had split by hand using a maul and wedges. Splitting wood was good exercise and a strength builder especially for one who sits in front of a keyboard most of the day.

Instead of starting the fire with the picture as he had planned earlier, he used corncobs saturated in melted wax from candle remnants. Later, he would toss in the picture when the fire was raging. He placed kindling on top of the cobs and then he arranged some hard maple, teepee fashion, over it all. Before Ginny had half of the table cleared, the fire had a good start, so he grabbed the drawing of the broken heart from behind the small stack of firewood and held it toward the open fire.

Immediately, he felt a burning pain in the left side of his chest. It was so intense his outreaching left arm, the one he was holding the drawing with, reacted as quickly as a knee tapped with a hammer.

"Jesus!" he said, loud enough for Ginny to hear.

"Everything all right?" she said from the kitchen. "Don't get burned."

"No, I'm okay," he was able to say.

As soon as his hand pulled the drawing back, the pain went away. He tried to place the drawing on the fire again, with the same results. He could not force his arm to obey the command to put the drawing in the fire, so he placed it back behind the stack of wood.

"Nice fire," she said emerging from the dining area. "What movie are we going to watch?"

"Pale Rider," he said. He knew that she liked Clint Eastwood westerns, and this was one that was not too bad. Besides, he hoped that they would not get as far as the middle before things happened. Things did happen, but not what he had planned for.

Chapter Four

With the fire started, and Ginny heading for the bathroom, he retrieved the picture from behind the stack of wood and took it down the open switchback stairway. At the bottom of the stairway and to the right was the access into the furnace room directly under the living room. He opened the door and placed the picture against the wall behind the water heater.

"I'll deal with you later," he said.

By the time he got back up the stairs, the fire had quickly caught and was burning with intensity. Ginny joined him in the living room and sat on the leather reclining sofa. She watched as he arranged oversized pillows on the Tinsing rug directly in front of the TV and alongside the fire.

There was a 48-inch HDTV mounted on rails so that it could be slid down to almost floor level. He had placed a wire-mesh screen in front of the fire so that none of the burning embers would pop out and ruin the oriental, hand-woven rug, named for the Tinsing province from where he had picked it up on a trip to China. The twelve-by-fifteen-foot rug had a blue border with the Chinese symbol for good luck in blue in the center on a field of wheat-colored wool. He had purchased the rug for a mere $1,100 at the factory on one of his many trips to the communist state shortly after President Nixon, in 1974, opened up the American tourism trade into the previously closed country. He had toured the factory where the rugs were made watching in awe as the Chinese women worked the loom by hand in dimly-lit unheated factories, threading each piece of wool using centuries-old methods. When the weaving was completed, hand-held shears sculpted the surface to give the woven images a 3-D look.

The factory had burned down years ago and was never rebuilt, making the rugs priceless. And to think he had intentions of seducing

Ginny on that very rug. He might have succeeded except when she joined him on the floor and they were snuggled amidst the middle of the pillows, the thumping started. He heard it first and knew exactly what it was, or at least where it was coming from. He tried to ignore the muffled sound hoping Ginny would not hear it.

"What's that?" she asked, raising her head up from the pillow.

"What?" he responded. As it became more noticeable the sound reminded him of Poe's *The Tell-Tale Heart*.

"That thumping." she said, "What's that thumping noise?"

"It's probably just the hot-water heating pump," he said, without conviction.

"It's like the bass drum in a marching band," she said. "I can feel it in my chest."

He could too, but he wasn't going to admit it.

Chapter Five

"I can't stand it," Ginny finally said. "Turn that pump thing off, or I'm going!"

"All right," he said, as he stood up facing away from her, trying to keep her from seeing the quickly disappearing bulge in his pants. Sitting upright, she pulled her legs up to her chest and wrapped her arms around her shins, resting her chin on her bent knees. She looked like a little girl pouting because she was being punished for something she had done wrong.

Readjusting his privates with his right hand, he headed down the stairs toward the furnace room and the thumping sound, which was now quite loud. He flicked on the light switch before opening the door and entering the room. Once inside he immediately closed the door for what he saw startled and scared him at the same time.

The picture was away from the wall and seemed to be standing on its own in the center of the room. Beside it lay a knife, a bowie knife used by hunters to gut their catch in the field allowing them to take the carcass back to camp. He had never used one, but recognized it as one similar to that used by his uncle to clean freshly-shot rabbits. His uncle also used his knife to remove the hide from deer and other animals. This one was shiny and sharp, catching every beam of light just as his uncle's had after he finished honing it before the hunt.

The knife, however, was not what raised goose bumps on his arms, but rather the picture itself. From the center of the picture where the heart was, there was thumping – thumping like a bass drum hit from the other side with its beater – aptly named as the heart appeared to be beating. The beats changed rhythm and started to sound as if the picture were talking, talking directly to him. Keeping his eyes glued to the scene, he cocked his head slightly to discern the words from the irregular beat. What he was able to make out from the thumping sounded like:

Kill! Kill! Kill! You must kill her. Kill! Kill! Kill! You must kill the bitch. The curse will be lifted, when you do this. Then it repeated the refrain. He felt as though the drum beats were taking over his mind and soul. He watched as if in a dream as his right arm reached out while he bent down and picked up the knife. When he stood up, his left arm reached for the door, turned the knob, and pushed it open. Sweat was running down his forehead and into his eyes, blurring his vision even further than the fog of the dream he thought he was in.

His feet plodded along, first through the door then across the lower level vinyl floor and then toward the stairs. When he got to the landing halfway up the stairs, he hesitated, concerned that Ginny would see him coming with the knife outstretched.

I must look like Norman Bates from Psycho, he thought to himself. Turning on the landing and heading up the second half-flight of stairs leading out of the lower level, he relaxed a little as he saw Ginny was facing away from him, still hugging her knees. He couldn't hear the thumping anymore, but that didn't mean it wasn't there. Maybe it had her hypnotized in the same way he seemed to be.

He was moving very slowly and not making any noise. In the darkened room, lit only by the fire and by two candles still burning on the kitchen table, he glided effortlessly, silently toward the unaware woman. He moved behind the double-reclining sofa so that he was directly behind her. In the next instant, he found himself kneeling down and reaching out to grab her hair with his left hand while his right placed the knife parallel with the floor and aimed directly at her long, thin neck.

"Ginger," he softly called out, using her real name instead of her nickname.

Startled, she lifted her head and dropped her hands from around her knees.

He was aware of the thumping again as he pulled her head back and sliced outwardly, first jabbing her in front of the Adam's apple and then slicing backward cutting her jugular. There was a gurgling sound as blood pumped in pulses from the open artery, some of it finding its way into her severed larynx, bubbling back in and out as she tried to breathe.

Kill her! *Kill her*! *Kill her*! The thumping seemed to say. He sliced one more time as her body quivered in her death throes. Still holding her half-severed head in his left hand, he slumped backward and collapsed into a coma-like sleep.

Chapter Six

The sound of a car woke him up. Opening his eyes, the bright light of day caused him to slam his eyelids closed again. He shook his head to clear the fog his mind was in. When he opened his eyes for the second time his hand closed tightly around something in his right hand. He lifted his hand into view and squinting in the bright light of day, he saw one of his Wüsthof knives blinding him with reflected sunlight.

Why am I holding a knife on the floor of the living room? he thought. Then the awareness of the night before slammed into his mind like a gallows trap door opening with a pull of a lever. He dropped the knife which fell onto the Pergo floor ringing with anger. He bolted upright and felt for the blood which he thought would be everywhere, but there was none. There was no blood and no Ginny.

"What the fuck!" he said aloud. "Where in the hell is she and what happened to the blood?"

The phone rang as he rolled over onto all fours and forced himself to stand. He staggered to the cordless phone on the end table next to the dual reclining sofa. Plopping down on the end of the sofa, he reached over and snagged the still clamoring instrument.

"Hello," he said, in a gruff morning voice.

"Hello back," Ginny said. "How is Mr. Pass-Out-On-The-Floor?"

"What?" he said. "What happened? Where are you?"

"I'm at home, silly," she said. "When you came back up from checking your water pump or whatever that noisy thingy was, you sat down behind me and the next thing I knew you were curled up on your side sound asleep. I watched the rest of the movie while you snored away behind me. I couldn't rouse you to get you to go to bed or even roll over from that fetal position you were in, so I came home. At least you got the thumping stopped, or I should say it quit on its own as soon as you started snoring."

"I'm really at a loss for words," he said. "How about another chance tonight?"

"No thanks," she said. "I've got another date tonight. You've really been on probation with me and last night kinda sent you back to jail as far as I'm concerned."

"Wait! Wait!" he shouted into the phone, but it was too late, she had already hung up. "That freakin' painting!" he added, speaking to the dial tone.

Later in the day he tried two other women he had dated before Ginny. They both were busy for the foreseeable future.

He went to his loft to write, one of the only loves left in his life. After two hours, he was still staring at only a paragraph of words on the LCD monitor.

"Damn!" he said aloud and slammed his fist on the corner of the desk. "I've got the worst writer's block I've ever had."

Normally the words would flow like diarrhea from his brain. He was proud of the fact that he couldn't type fast enough to get his thoughts into the computer. If he got to a stopping point on a novel he would change venue by switching over to a short story, a poem, or a children's story. There was always something flowing from his imagination. He decided to give up and take a nap.

When he awoke that evening he felt really alone and a little depressed. He started hitting the wine and was halfway through a second bottle of moscato d'asti, a sweet, after dinner wine he had been saving for a romantic dinner, when the thumping started again.

"Goddamn it!" he said, slurring the words badly. "I'm gettin' rid of that friggin' paintin' for good."

Stumbling to the basement and opening the door to the little utility room where he had last seen the painting, he had to close his eyes and open them three times before what he saw registered in his nearly-pickled mind.

Sitting cross-legged on the cement floor in front of him was what could only be described as an American Indian. The man was dressed in buckskin top and pants, both with shredded strips of skin at each seam. On his head, dividing his forehead into a top and bottom, was a black band of leather holding his hair back, and on his feet were dark brown moccasins. He was the stereotype of Jay Silverheels as Tonto from the Lone Ranger TV series he had seen as a child. All he needed to do was grunt and say "Ugh, Kimosabe!" If Scout, Tonto's horse was outside, it would be a complete picture.

All the writer could do was say, "uh."

"Biligani-ashki, tkin-cid-da-hi," the Indian said, in a foreign language the writer was not familiar with. He repeated the words again, "White boy, sit down!"

Although the words were still foreign to him, he somehow understood every word as if he were sitting at a chair in the U.N. with a translator whispering in his ear.

It was more of a command than a request so the writer sat down, not cross-legged as the Indian, but with his knees up and in front of him and his back resting against the wall. The Indian then reached out and rested his hands, palm up on his knees and closed his eyes as if drifting off to some foreign land.

"Listen," the translator whispered in his ear.

"There was a brave who lived long ago with the ancient people. He became of age when he touched his first bear with his bare hands. This was a very brave thing which had only been done by a very few. Most of them went to the happy hunting ground put there by the same bear. Only a handful lived."

Happy hunting ground! Did they really talk like that, the writer thought? *Maybe the translator could only find those words to describe what the Indian meant in his language.*

"Touching the bear was what his great-great grandfather had done to earn the name Sate-pa-hoodle, he who touches bear. The brave was proving that he was worthy of his family name. The next summer the young brave killed a mountain lion with only his knife. In so doing, he received deep scratches across his back from the lion's claws, the scars which he wore with pride. He killed an eagle with an arrow that same summer. We all thought he would be chief some day, but he had other ideas.

"Although many squaws wanted him to choose them as his wife, two years before he had promised only one that she would be his bride. It was thought that their offspring would become as brave as he and contribute greatly to the welfare of the tribe. But the brave acts with the bear, the lion, and the eagle, made him proud and selfish. He announced to the tribe that he did not need anyone anymore.

"'I am the bravest man on earth. I am going to be a great god so I must be on my own. I do not need anyone else to help me.'

"'But I have made you a bonnet from the eagle feathers for you to wear on our wedding day,' his betrothed pleaded. 'From the lion I have rendered the fat for our wedding ceremony and tanned the hide for our wedding bed.'

"'That is not my concern,' he told her."

That said, the squatting Indian continued, "He went away from the tribe taking his enormous pride with him and leaving a broken-hearted, crying bride behind, one that he had already defiled. No one else would want her because she was not pure and for fear that he would come back and claim her."

"Why are you telling me this?" the writer asked. His words came out in that foreign tongue as if he were fluent in the language.

"You are like that brave in that you have not honored your obligation to your people. A promise is a promise and should not be broken unless released by the one the promise is made to."

"Are you talking about that stupid picture?" the writer said, looking and waving his hand about, trying to indicate what he did not see in the room.

"Among others," the Indian said. "You have been selfish as the foolish brave was and have used others for your own gain and pleasure without concern."

"So, what happened to the brave?" he asked, rather smugly, and out of curiosity.

"It is you who must finish the story," the Indian said. "It will be your ending."

He was starting to sober up now and his head was hurting and eyes burning. He rubbed his forehead and then closed his eyes to finish the massage. When he opened his eyes he was staring at not the Indian, but the picture instead. The Indian was gone. The thumping started again and this time, more than before, he could feel it in his chest.

Instead of destroying the picture as he intended to do, he gingerly picked it up and carried it upstairs to his loft. He set the picture behind his desk on a worktable, resting it against the wall. The thumping continued so that he could hear it inside his ears and, without touching, feel it in his chest. His head, too, was throbbing in rhythm with the picture and his own heart.

"It's just a hangover," he commented aloud as he turned to look out the window, but somehow he didn't believe it.

Over the maple trees to the east, the sky was starting to reflect the suns rising, signaling the start of a new day.

He went to the kitchen and readied a pot of coffee, adding two extra scoops of grounds to make it stronger. As he waited for the coffee to finish percolating, he stared at the lightening sky and thought about the "dream" he had just had.

"It must have been a dream," he said.

As he poured the first cup of strong coffee he clutched his throbbing chest. Fighting back nausea, he returned to the loft, sat at his desk, and sipped the stimulating liquid. Before he finished the first cup, he was writing a check to the artist, double what she had asked for. As he sealed the check in an envelope and placed a stamp on it, he felt a warm sensation pass through his body. The throbbing in his chest seemed to diminish somewhat, not a whole lot, but just enough to be detectable.

"Thank God the coffee's working," he said. He wrote two more checks that day and four more the next. Each went to different charities from which he had received numerous requests for money. With each one the throbbing was less and less.

Days later, he was working on a new book, the proceeds of which he vowed to give away, when the phone rang.

"Hello," he said.

"Hi," someone sheepishly said on the other end. "It's me, Ginny." She didn't have to say her name; he recognized her voice at once. "I'm so sorry," she said. Will you give me another chance? I can come over tonight."

His heart was thumping again, but the picture was not the cause this time.

The Undulating Mass

It really was a dark and stormy night — well, it was raining at least.

Slowly I crept down the poorly-lit wooden steps, down into the basement of "Yellow Hell." Even though I had turned on the lights at the top of the stairs, the three forty-watt bulbs mounted in the ceiling at different locations barely cast shadows into the pit that was the below-grade level of the one story house off Cleveland Avenue in Shaftsbury, Vermont. What little light the bulbs gave off that was able to penetrate the densely packed spider webs hanging from the exposed floor joists, was absorbed by the black mold that clung to the concrete block walls like stepped-on dog poop to a new pair of jogging shoes. This was why I carried a strong flashlight with me during all my sojourns into the bowels of Yellow Hell.

Yellow Hell was the affectionate name that my wife and I gave to the rental house, which is what we had settled on in a futile effort to find affordable, decent housing in rural Vermont. We were building a new home and there were no alternatives, affordable or otherwise, which would give us a nine-month lease while the house was under construction. The outside of the rental home was painted a dingy yellow, hence the nickname. The inside walls were painted in several layers of blue in order to cover up successive encroachments of the same, basement-dwelling black mold, which had crept through the basement ceiling and into the living areas above.

The basement was its own pure hell. A sump pump barely kept up with the water oozing through the foundation walls and into a trench that ringed the perimeter of the fifty-by-fifty-foot enclosure. Once, in a half-hearted attempt to clean the space, I had found a child's small toy boat in one of the trenches. What child was mad enough to play in that slime infested bilge water, I could only hazard a guess. The sump pump was in a pit at the low end of the basement and when it was

46

on, sounded like a flushing toilet. In dry weather it turned on every ninety seconds and, during heavy rains, it ran continuously. Coupled with the inadequate, constantly running dehumidifier, the din in the basement was like a bad one-man band playing a John Philip Sousa marching song, day and night or 24/7 as merchants like to say. Some days I could even hear the water flowing in the trenches like rapids in the Colorado River.

During heavy rains, more than an inch in a day, the sump pump could not keep up and the basement flooded. In addition to the moisture encroaching from the outside, the sewer vents, instead of being routed up to the roof, opened into the ceiling space between the spider-webbed joists. More than once, the aging septic system had backed up dumping raw sewage onto the floor and into the trench. All of the moisture and fecal matter was the source of food for the enormous growth of mold. It was a thick, furry accumulation that reached up from the walls of the basement and enveloped the entire house. It clung to the insulation between the plaster and the outside siding like millions of bats in a cave. The mold was its own entity, growing, living, waiting.

It was for these reasons that I was more than apprehensive when I made my way down the stairs for my weekly inspection of the basement. The inspection was to make sure that the sump pump's drain hose was still connected to the pipe that penetrated the exterior wall. I also checked that the dehumidifier fins were not covered with ice or that its drain hose that dumped into the nearest trench was not clogged with mold.

I squinted as my eyes adjusted to the dimly-lit room. Although the sun outside Yellow Hell was shining brightly between high cumulus clouds, not many of its rays were able to penetrate the basement windows. It was as if the mold, like Dracula, could not survive the light of day and somehow it caused a film to form on the glass to dim the natural light.

As my vision became more accustomed to the darkness, my eyes were drawn toward the darkest part of the basement, the southwest corner, where I could sense, more than see, a presence. I aimed the flashlight in that direction and squeezed my eyelids tighter, for even the battery-powered beam of the flashlight seemed to be absorbed by the subterranean growth. But what I discovered nestled up against the wall was large enough to be easily seen. Its movement was discernable from the surrounding inanimate objects I had not yet removed to the junk pile behind the garage. I blinked, not once, but twice in disbelief, for in front of me was a dark, large, three-foot square, undulating mass. It rose ten inches above the damp concrete floor and seemed to sway to the cacophony of the flushing pump and the pulsating drone of the straining dehumidifier.

Cautiously, I approached the square blob, which reminded me of the 1958 movie with that name. Unlike the ill-fated farmer in the beginning of the movie (who was absorbed by the mass when he stuck a stick in it), I was not going to be the first one to provoke it by jabbing at it, even if I had had a stick. As my eyes adjusted further and enough light filtered in from the windows, I could see white objects protruding from the top of the mass. One step closer, revealed the white objects to be mushrooms, dancing on the waving mass like corks on a blackened sea. I moved to my right, and it seemed as though the mushrooms were following my movement like the many eyes on a large insect.

I moved no closer as the droning dehumidifier and flushing noise seemed to encourage the mass to move. I was sure it was inching its way toward me as I slowly backed toward the stairs. The eyes of the mass were staring and unblinking. It seemed to be hungry for a taste of my flesh.

Backing up further, I nearly tripped on the bottom slat of the steps, catching myself with my free left hand. The mass seemed to laugh at my misstep. I was sure it was capable of leaping should I falter in my quest to leave its lair. I backed up the stairs, and although I no longer could see it, I kept my vision trained in its direction. I was positive that it was watching me and was still swaying back and forth, awaiting another chance.

It wasn't until I had reached the top step, and had backed safely through the cellar door, that I dared to turn around. I headed for the kitchen sink where I kept a spray bottle filled with half bleach and half water. The bottle was used to sterilize the aboveground living spaces whenever I saw the mold creeping through the several layers of paint. The window cleaner that had come with the spray bottle had already been used in an attempt to remove several years of dirt from Yellow Hell's half-century old windows.

Once armed with my pungent concoction, I proceeded to re-enter the cellar stairs with the squirter bottle in my right hand and the flashlight in my left. I knew no mold could stand the deadly effects of good old chlorine bleach. So that I would not succumb to the fumes from the bleach, I pulled my T-shirt collar up and over my nose. As I slowly descended into the hole, the high-pitched noise from the creaking stairs echoed my heartbeat, which was thumping loudly in my chest and throbbing in my neck.

My right arm was stretched out at full length, my fingers were clenched tightly around the squirter trigger, and my thumb gripped the neck of the bottle as I slowly approached. In cop-like fashion, I held the flashlight straight out parallel with my chest and away from my body. In this way, should the mass launch a counter attack, its wrath would be directed toward the light, missing my body.

As I inched closer, the dehumidifier shut off and, with the pump between flushes, an eerie hush fell over the room. It was the calm before the storm, the quiet before the battle, the pall before the death rattle. My shoes squished on the damp concrete. There was no turning back, no surprise attack. The battle lines were drawn.

The air was heavy with moisture as I got within squirting distance and I panicked, not knowing if I had set the tip of the squirter for spray or stream. I would just have to take my chances and hope it was on stream. Even if there was enough light to check, I was not going to take my eyes off the mass, which was now in full view. The mushroom eyes watched me warily as I approached. The mass was growing larger in the dim light as if it were puffing itself up like a bullfrog to look larger than it really was. It became still and seemed to be leaning back like a rattlesnake poised for a strike, only there was no warning rattle.

Aiming carefully at the closest mushroom grouping, I took a deep breath and held it. My heart was still pounding in my chest as I took the first squeeze. A stream of liquid death issued forth from the tip of the bottle. I re-aimed and squirted again. Just then, the sump pump turned on and the dehumidifier started as if they were both cheering a Roman gladiator fighting a lion. I continued squirting again, and again, and again, back stepping toward the stairs with each pull on the trigger. I could swear I heard the mass screaming in agony, melting and acting as if it were the Wicked Witch of the West in the Wizard of Oz when she was hit with a stream of water. As I got closer to the stairs, I was glad that I had held my breath, for the mass was attacking. Not fooled at all by the angled light, it attacked with spores shot directly toward the stream of burning death.

By now I needed air badly, but was not about to take a breath in that dungeon. I turned and raced up the stairs hoping I had dealt a deathblow to the mass. My lungs were burning for fresh air as I reached the top of the stairs. I took in great gulps on the other side of the basement entrance door. It was then that I could smell the spores, which had enveloped me from behind and had followed me up from the basement. I closed the cellar door, stopping the wave of Black Death from entering the rest of the house. When I could breathe again normally, I looked at the nearly empty squirter bottle and turned off the flashlight. I set them both on the floor and went outside for fresh air and a much needed rest on the back porch stairs.

It was days before I mustered up the courage to return to the basement. By now I was eager to see what damage I had done to the mass. The overhead lights appeared to be brighter, and the beam from the flashlight illuminated more of the space than before, or so it seemed. I cautiously approached the battle zone ready to retreat should I need to re-arm myself with more bleach. But it was not necessary, for the mass was gone. In its place was what remained of a cardboard box that I had previously flattened and had forgotten to remove. Cardboard, I recalled, is made up mostly of cellulose, which is food for plant life, including mold. The collapsed box had been a very rich garden for the black mold and mushrooms, and they had grown very quickly in the damp environment.

A few days later, I continued my bleach assault on the black mold on the basement walls and removed any other source of mold food. When our new house was completed and we moved out at the end of the nine-month lease, I took pride in the fact that the basement was relatively clean and mold free.

My stay in Vermont only lasted another three years. As I headed for my new home in Ohio, I drove past the old house and noticed that Yellow Hell was still there. I wondered if the mold had returned.

The Insider Spider

It was a dark and stormy night!

Diane had just finished cleaning the basement, "Hoover-ing" all the cobwebs and spider skeletons into a disposable vacuum bag along with all the unfortunate live spiders and their nasty egg sacks, or so she thought!

"God, I hate spiders!" she said as she took off her cleaning clothes.

She took the vacuum, bag and all, climbed the stairs out from the dark, damp, dingy, arachnid-infested cellar and closed the door behind her. Standing in the corridor between the cellar door and the entrance to the kitchen she put everything she had worn into a plastic bag to fumigate later with a bug bomb. The dust mask she had over her face, the one-piece work suit, the T-shirt, the shoes and socks, the scarf that covered her reddish-blond hair, and the gloves all which protected her entire body from head to toe were crammed into the Glad, puncture-proof, contractor-strength bag, and sealed with duct tape. Even her underpants and meager bra were tossed into the bag. Naked, she opened the door to the attached garage and tossed the bag in the general direction of the trash can.

Still naked, she pushed the vacuum to the living room and unzipped the compartment which held the bag. Even though it was only half full, she tossed the bag into the still smoldering fireplace. The red-hot embers caused the bag to immediately burst into flames.

"Take that!" she shouted as she closed the glass doors sealing the inferno from the rest of the house.

It was then that she thought she heard a shrill sound as if a thousand tiny souls screamed in unison. She shook her head to clear the cobwebs (and egg sacks) from her mind and exited the living room.

"God, I hate spiders!" she said again and made her way to the bathroom and a nice hot shower to wash away any remnants of creepy-crawly things from the basement.

She had put off doing the cleaning job as long as possible until she related her arachnophobia to a friend. A friend who immediately told her, "You're never more than three feet from a spider." She didn't want to hear that and soon the words stuck to her mind like a fly in a web. Over and over, like an earworm, a song you hear on the morning radio show and can't get out of your head the rest of the day, the phrase played for days.

"Three feet! Three feet! You're never more than three feet."

It even had rhythm to it like a childhood taunt. Just like sucking all the gossamer strands from between the floor joists which comprised the ceiling of her basement, the tune was pulled out of her mind as she cleaned away.

The hot shower had a soothing as well as a cleansing effect on her body and mind. It was just after ten at night. Four hours she had worked on cleaning the basement. Four hours it took, but to her, it was worth the effort. Her skin was warm and red from the near scalding streams of steamy water. She would have taken a bath, but wanted to get her hair scrubbed too. She dried her hair with the hair dryer and used it to clear the mist from the mirror so she could see herself in it.

Satisfied, she headed for the comfort of her bed, one she had hoped to share, but tonight she was alone. She allowed herself three of the dark chocolate Hershey's kisses that she kept in a dish on the night stand next to her queen-sized feather bed. The kisses were one of her only vices and they reminded her of a forbidden lover. Turning off the night light, she crawled under the sheets, grabbed the full-length body pillow, and put her arms and legs around it, hugging it tightly for comfort.

No more spiders, she thought. *No more spiders just three feet below me, beneath the bedroom floor nestled in the ceiling of the basement.*

She slept.

Awakened by a noise, one Diane was all too familiar with, one that sounded eerie hearing it from the comfort of her bedroom, she opened her eyes wide. She was still cuddling the pillow, and pulled it tightly against her for safety. *That noise*, she thought. *That noise sounds like the treadmill running.* She had the treadmill in the basement and used it often. She always dreaded using it in the nasty basement, but had no choice since there was no other room to put it in her small house. Also, the basement stayed cooler than the rest of the house which kept her from overheating in the summer while she did her near-daily exercise routine. The thought that she was surrounded by spiders less than three feet away on all sides had prompted her to start the cleaning.

It was the treadmill. She was sure of it.

"How did it turn itself on?" She said aloud.

Only the treadmill did not turn itself on. In the back of her mind the taunt started anew sounding like the tiny little screams from the fireplace.

"Three feet! Three feet! You're never more than three feet."

"Wait a minute!" she exclaimed. "Where is Johnnye."

Normally one of her cats crawled into bed with her sometime in the middle of the night. Her other cat, Reaper, was usually aloof and slept alone in some unusual place like the sink basin in the spare bathroom.

"Here Johnnye, here kitty," she called out."

The cat did not come running as it usually did when she called. The last time she had seen them both was when she had started cleaning in the basement. The cat's litter box was in the basement near the bottom of the stairs. When the door was closed to the basement, as she was sure she had done when she had finished the four-hour cleaning session, the cats used a hinged flap in the basement door to get to the litter box.

When she had brought out the vacuum, they both bolted up the stairs away from the noisy machine even before she turned it on. She couldn't recall if they had returned or not, but they could have done so to use the litter box while she was taking her shower. But by now, Johnnye would have been in bed with her. She squinted at the alarm clock and saw that it was twelve thirteen. The noise from the treadmill was still coming up through the floor.

Maybe, she thought, *the cats had gone downstairs to investigate the noise.* They usually stayed away from the treadmill when she used it, but they did watch her with that why-the-hell-do-you-want-to-do-that look that cats sometimes give their owners.

She listened again in hopes that the noise might be someone driving by the house on the busy road she lived on, but no, it was the treadmill. There was something different this time about the sound the treadmill made. Something different than what she heard when her "friend" used it on one of his not-frequent-enough visits to see her. From her kitchen, when he used the treadmill, she could hear the rhythmic shoom-shoom-shoom-shoom as the motor responded to the impact of each of his steps.

This sound however was Shoom-shoom…shoom-shoom…shoom-shoom…shoom-shoom then a pause, and then it started over again. The four sets of two steps repeated the gallop almost as if four people were on the treadmill, or something with four legs, two sets on each side. She had shivers as she tried to remember if a spider had six legs or eight. She had avoided looking at the spider skeletons hanging from their death webs as she vacuumed them so couldn't picture the number of legs they had.

Deciding to investigate (did she have a choice?) she threw the blanket aside and slipped her feet into her soft bunny shoes she kept beside the bed. Squish! She felt something give way against the toes of her right foot as soon as she stood to walk. There was a sensation of wiggling and wet inside and against her foot as she sat back down on the bed, reached over to the nightstand, and turned on the lamp. She pulled the booty off and found a yellowish-green and gooey mess.

"Yuck!" she said as she looked at the contents squished against her foot.

With her right hand, she pulled a tissue from the Kleenex box and wiped the pulverized glob from her foot being sure to clean what looked like fur caught between her toes. With her left hand, she reached across and picked up her reading glasses which were also on the nightstand, and put them on to exam the contents of the Kleenex.

"Three feet! Three feet! You're never more than three feet." Only this time the encounter was a lot closer than three feet.

"Well, that answers that question," she said aloud. "Eight legs!"

It was obviously a spider that must have crawled into her slippers right after she had taken them off when she crawled into bed. What looked like fuzz was eight black furry legs about the size of toothpicks.

It must have been looking for a warm place to spend the night, she thought.

"Johnnye," she said as she saw, or thought she saw, a dark object dart between the bed and the footlocker that was at the foot of the bed.

But there was no response.

Shoom-shoom…shoom-shoom…shoom-shoom…shoom-shoom came the sound from the basement, bringing her back to the reason she was awake in the middle of the night. She walked around the bed this time in her bare feet, checking to see if the cat was crouching where she saw the movement, but found no cat. Opening the closet door, she put on her spare pair of fuzzy slippers. She headed out of the bedroom and down the hall past the small office where she kept her computer, then out through the kitchen to the cellar door flipping on lights as she went.

"Oh no!" she exclaimed when she saw the hinged flap the cats used for access to the basement.

It looked as if someone was decorating for Halloween with fake cobwebs, only these were much more realistic.

The door the cats used was covered in shiny silky strands so that there was no way it could be opened, at least not without getting caught up in the stuff. This could explain why Johnnye was not in bed with her. She hoped the cats were okay, but feared the worst as the noise got louder from the basement. Shoom-shoom…shoom-shoom…shoom-shoom…shoom-shoom.

She did not own a gun, nor even a big knife, but she went back into the kitchen for the only weapon she could think of, a marble rolling pin, the one she had used the other day to make a pie for the church pot-luck dinner. It was heavy and if nothing else worked, she could at least look threatening to whatever was using the treadmill.

Shoom-shoom…shoom-shoom…shoom-shoom…shoom-shoom. The noise became even louder than before, as she turned the knob to the door and opened it ever so slightly. Again her peripheral vision caught the movement of some cat-sized object, this time from the kitchen – near the refrigerator. She did not call out for her cat this time. She had a feeling it would be futile.

Shoom-shoom…shoom-shoom…shoom-shoom…shoom-shoom. As she peered into the blackness of the basement from the slowly opening door, she could see a reddish glow emanating from the side of the basement where the treadmill was. Her first thought was to close the door, run to the phone, and call a friend, any friend, or at least call 911.

She had called 911 last year to report what she thought was a neighbor peering in through her bedroom window. He was a bit of a letch and had made suggestive comments to her when he had come to help her with her yard work. She paid him when he helped, but he wasn't interested in the money. When the police arrived, they found a branch from her pine tree had broken loose and was brushing up against the window making the noise she thought was the neighbor. She saw the policemen snickering as they headed back toward their cruiser and was embarrassed beyond words. Everyone in this small town knew everyone else and the pine-branch episode, which it became known as, was the talk of the town for days afterwards. She did not want add to it with a spider-on-the treadmill caper. Therefore, she would investigate herself.

Shoom-shoom…shoom-shoom…shoom-shoom…shoom-shoom. The noise brought her back to the reality of her little house. The reddish glow from the basement became more noticeable as her eyes adjusted to the dimmer light beyond the basement door. She could make out the backside of the hinged cat door and it too was covered in the web-like material only from this side it caught the red glow and seemed to absorb it and quiver as if it were on fire. She knew if she bent down and touched the stuff it would stick to her hand. She shuddered at the thought of cobwebs clinging to her body and not being able to get them all off fast enough.

Shoom-shoom…shoom-shoom…shoom-shoom…shoom-shoom. The red light flickered in unison with the rhythm of the noise. It reminded her of the red light hanging from the back of a caboose that she had seen at night when she was a little girl. Her upstairs bedroom window had been across the tracks from the train station. When the train pulled slowly away, the light, hung by the conductor, had swung slowly from side to side beaming rays of light through her bedroom window. That had been a pleasant light; but what was coming from the basement was a lot more ominous.

Shoom-shoom…shoom-shoom…shoom-shoom…shoom-shoom. The cellar door made a creak as she opened it and the noise stopped. She froze, halfway through the door and held her breath. The noise had stopped, but the glowing light was still there only it was steady and brighter as if it were aimed in her direction. She decided to bend over and peer deeper into the basement. Maybe she could see far enough to make out what was using the treadmill. The light still seemed to be aimed in her direction as she crouched low and got to her knees. Still clutching the rolling pin so tightly her knuckles were turning white, she leaned forward using her hands to support her.

As she stretched out horizontally, she could make out more of the web-like material attached to the floor. As more of the basement came into view, lit by the beacon of red light, she saw that the web stretched from the floor to the ceiling. It could only be called a web as it radiated outward from the center and was attached in several places to the floor and the ceiling. In the center of the web was a cocoon like mass that looked like a giant fly that had been wrapped to be a spider's next meal. The mass was wiggling and in the eerie red glow, she could make out an object protruding outside of the cocoon.

She squinted and concentrated her gaze on the object. No, it couldn't be! But it was. It was Johnnye's rabies tag, one of the ones she got from the vet during the cats' annual checkup and immunization treatments. Her beloved cat had been wrapped up for dinner by a giant spider.

Infuriated, she stood up and raced down the stairs, so angry she didn't even turn on the overhead lights to the basement. Rolling pin raised high she was ready for a fight, but was stopped dead in her tracks on the last step frozen by what she saw.

It was the eyes. The eyes had stopped her before she had gotten to the basement floor. Forget the fact that she was staring at a spider the size of a large dog. Forget the fact that this thing from beyond hell was standing on her treadmill facing her with fangs and soda-straw like appendages coming out of its mouth; a mouth that does not chew, but only sucks the liquid out of its prey. It was the red eyes staring at her without blinking that kept her immobile. Staring at her like the headlights on a car about ready to run her down.

"Jesus Christ," she said aloud.

She couldn't remember the last time she had used the Lord's name in vain. Perhaps it was when as a youngster as her ice-skates case smacked her in the face, bloodying her lip. That accident had required six stitches to close, leaving a permanent scar which caused her to talk with a lisp similar to her favorite actor, Humphrey Bogart. Perhaps she had uttered those words when she had stepped in a pothole in a dark parking lot and fell hitting her face and injuring the same lip. It didn't matter; she meant the cuss word this time. Those red spider eyes were penetrating, hypnotizing, foreboding, mesmerizing.

"Where in the hell did it come from?" she asked of no one. "It must have been living down in the basement a long time, but what did it eat?"

Not the cat food, she thought. *Spiders can only eat liquids and some small amounts of predigested flesh*, she remembered from biology class. *Yuck, predigested flesh from secretions they inject with those soda-straws and fangs sticking out of their mouths.*

So what did it survive on? This was a question she would have to answer some other time, for the spider started to move, jarring her from the trance those eyes had put her in.

The spider was turning away from her momentarily, diverting its eyes so that she was no longer frozen on the stairway. Remembering why she had come down with such fury in the first place, she turned toward the web with the cocooned cat. She darted over to the closest strand and took a whack with the rolling pin knocking the web free from the ceiling joist. She kicked at the web stuck to the floor and grimaced as it gave way, sticking to her slipper. She then smacked the next strand and kicked the next until the web fell and the cocoon bounced off of the floor. A paw emerged from the mass and started to flail at the air.

The cat would have to fend for itself as she turned her attention once again toward the treadmill and its gruesome occupant. The spider had turned completely away from her and was lowering its head to the front of the treadmill at the same time raising its rear; she recalled it was actually called an abdomen, the part of the spider that the web is secreted from. Just to prove the point the spider shot out a strand of the gooey silk which missed her, but hit and attached to the banister to her right. Just as she dodged to avoid that strand, another came at her more directly, hitting her in the right shoulder. This time she swung the rolling pin but it got caught in another strand which was aimed directly toward her face.

She dodged another that went out over the top of her head and stuck to the ceiling. Heading for what looked like a safety zone behind the dryer, she crouched just in time to avoid a shot to her left leg. Now the ropey strands were crisscrossing the basement glowing in the red light of the eyes which reflected off the white paint of the concrete block basement walls. She didn't know what to do next. The rolling pin was ineffective so she looked around searching for another weapon.

Bleach! There was a container of bleach on the shelf above the washer. She would have to stand up and reach over the dryer to get to it, but what choice did she have. Without much more thought, she stood up and reached out for the bleach container catching her right ear and right arm on a sticky strand of the web. The spider did not stop. He continued shooting strands of the milky liquid in all directions which solidified as soon as it hit the air sticking to whatever was in its path.

She crouched back down behind the dryer and opened the lid of the plastic gallon jug of bleach. *Now what?* she thought. *How can I get the bleach on that thing out there?* The only way was to get close enough to be able to splash some on it. She didn't even know if it would have an effect, but if she could get it in the spider's eyes, those red headlights, it might do some damage to the beast. As she contemplated running at the spider while it was facing the opposite direction to get to the eyes, she saw the two beacons of red light moving across the opposite wall from right to left.

The spider must be turning back towards me, she thought. *Now how can I run at it and avoid those fangs? Maybe I could pour the bleach in my slippers and toss them at the creature. Even if I just come close it might splash in its eyes blinding it. I have no other option.*

She remembered a story a friend who had lived on a tropical island had told her about an arachnid he had encountered on the side of his house. It was the size of his hand and looked particularly dangerous. He went into the house, got a can of bug spray, and returned to find the spider in the same spot.

Taking careful aim, he sprayed towards the spider and backed away to watch it die. What it did however was jump at him, spread its legs like a parachute, and with great skill glided with deadly aim right toward his face. He was able to dodge the flying bug eater and made a beeline for his front door. He later got up enough courage to go looking for the thing and found it not far from its death leap, its legs curled in toward its body forming a near perfect furry ball. Placing it in a glass mason jar he had taken it to an entomologist friend of his. He was informed that it was a wolf spider which can get quite large.

"It runs its prey down, and can even glide in from the top of a tree with excellent accuracy to bite unsuspecting prey," the entomologist had said.

"Tell me about it," he had replied, shivers running down his back.

"What you got here is a not a poisonous spider," the entomologist had continued. "But its bite could cause you to end up in the hospital for several days; that is if you were found in time and weren't bitten in a lethal spot."

Lethal spot, she thought. What is a lethal spot and is this a wolf spider? She remembered her friend telling her they did not usually spin webs but can spin cocoons like the one surrounding Johnnye. *Usually*?

Johnnye! She thought about the cat lying on the floor when she leaped behind the dryer. *My poor Johnnye*! *No time to worry about the cat.*

She took off her slippers and poured bleach into each one, enough to saturate the shoe and all its fuzzy fur. The smell of chlorine immediately filled her nostrils with a burning sensation.

As the red lights stopped moving on the wall behind her, she stood up and tossed her right slipper directly at the monster's face.

Splat! It made a wet sound missing its mark, hitting the spider above its right eye, but bleach poured from the slipper and into the eye. One red headlight went out and the basement filled with a guttural scream, not high pitched but low and rumbling. She was holding the other slipper in her right hand and gave it a mighty heave making a direct hit in the left eye. The second light went out, but the thing crouched low and leapt, right for her. She ducked just as she saw the dark shadow come down the stairs and head in her direction.

"Oh no" she said, but her cry was drowned out by the braying spider.

There must be another one, she thought. Before she ducked down she saw the cocoon lying limply on the floor. *Johnnye must have gotten out.*

She found the rolling pin on the floor and grabbed it as tightly as she could, ready to use it if given the chance. Suddenly, the dryer crashed into her – moved by the force of the spider as it came down hard against it. She was knocked backwards against the wall pinning her there unable to move. She lost her grip on the rolling pin and it fell to the cement floor breaking off one of the handles.

I'm going to die! she thought. *I'm going to be eaten by an angry spider.*

She imagined its fangs sinking into her neck, paralyzing and immobilizing her. She would then be wrapped in a cocoon, kept alive for a future feast. A feast for a beast using those long soda-straws sunk deeply into her flesh sucking the life out of her bit by bit until she lost consciousness.

She looked up and saw that the red headlights were not completely out, but only dimmed by the bleach. They were now directly over her on top of the dryer and peering down at the trapped prey. The spider's mouth opened and pincher like appendages on either side of its mouth reached down to grasp her head so that the fangs could do their job. She could feel heat from its mouth raining down on her. It was not its breath, for spiders do not breathe the way mammals do. It smelled putrefying, like the black mold which grew on the basement walls before she had the drainage around the outside of the house fixed. She was so mesmerized by the eyes, she could not even scream.

And then it happened!

As it neared within inches of grabbing her by the neck, something, the dark shadow she had seen before, leapt up from the cellar floor onto the spider's head. The spider reared back and howled, a goose bump-raising howl that broke the hypnotizing spell of those red eyes. When the spider pushed back from the wall with its front legs, the dryer went with it allowing her to wiggle free from where she had been wedged between it and the cellar wall.

She heard the spider hit the floor, red lights from the eyes bouncing off the ceiling and walls like the flashing of a cop car's emergency lights. She moved to her left and stuck her head out to see what was going on and at the same time her right hand found the remaining handle of the rolling pin. Her mouth dropped open and her eyes widened as she saw Johnnye on the spider's back sinking his teeth into the connecting tissue between the spider's head and thorax.

Reaper was on the spider's head clawing at the eyes. Reaper had to have been the dark shadow that followed her from her bedroom to the basement; the cat that would run and hide whenever a stranger visited; the cat that jumped a foot in the air when she tossed the Sunday paper on the floor; the cat that slept in the spare bathroom with one eye open, had turned out to be much more courageous than she could ever have imagined.

She pushed herself up, and wielding the broken rolling pin, joined in the fracas smashing the spider in the area of the mouth. One of the fangs broke loose and fell to the floor and she bashed some more. Meanwhile the cats were clawing and biting the thing unmercifully, especially Johnnye who had been wrapped in the cocoon minutes earlier. She knew the cat hated being put in the pet carrier for the annual trip to the vet and fought like hell to stay free. Being placed in a cocoon must have pissed him off royally and now he was wreaking vengeance on the thing that had put him there.

Johnnye's teeth must have found the nerve that connected the head to the rest of the body, just like when cats catch a mouse and are done playing with it, dispensing its life with a single bite. The spider went limp, the light from the eyes went out, and it rolled onto its side. She kept hitting it until it finally curled up in a ball, liquids spilling from its torn neck and punctured eyes. Both she and the cats collapsed onto the floor breathing heavily. The spider did not move, but to be sure, she reached out and kicked it with her bare foot. Nothing happened.

Epilog

This basement cleanup took almost as long as the first one only Diane couldn't use a vacuum to suck up the web and spider. All of that mess went into Glad bags by hands protected with rubber gloves. The spider, although large in size, surprisingly did not weigh a lot. *It must be all hair and skeleton, more menacing than substance*, she thought.

She wasn't going to call anyone about this even though she had the evidence. Instead, she dispensed with the mess in the fireplace adding more kindling and a couple of logs to make sure it completely turned to ash. The events of the night would be a secret she and the cats would take to their graves. She kept the one fang that had been knocked loose in the struggle for a trophy, but would show it to no one. The opening the spider had evidently used to access the basement was an old coal chute in the corner of the basement, left from when before the furnace had been converted to gas. She thought it had been sealed shut, but it must have been knocked open by the spider. All the thing had to do was squeeze its main mass through the opening, drawing its legs close to its body until it was in the house. She boarded the opening up as soon as she was done cleaning. The spider must have decided to use the treadmill to draw her down to its trap after concluding that the cat would not be enough food.

She rewarded the cats with a can of tuna, their favorite food, and all three of them, exhausted, fell asleep on the couch in front of the funeral pyre. "Thank God that's over," she said before she closed her eyes.

Or was it?

"Three feet! Three feet! You're never more than three feet."

Bob's Last Ride

It was a dark and stormy night.

No storm yet, but it was dark and a storm was on its way. Bob had just experienced a nasty "ENDO," as biker's call it, and the pain shooting through his right knee and both wrists was approaching unbearable. ENDO is short for end over, which is the act of going over your handlebars. ENDO happens when only the front brakes are used, or, if an object like a pothole stops your bike faster than your body.

Bob had ridden through the cemetery many times, but not this late in the evening. The sun went down fast in late October in Ohio, especially when blocked by a band of thick dark clouds in the west. A cold front was fast approaching and threatened to drop temperatures at least 30 degrees with its passage. It had been sunny and warm, in the upper 60's, when Bob had gotten home from work. Deciding to take advantage of the rare, warm fall day, he had gone by himself like he did on most of his late afternoon bike rides.

Man, this weather is nice, he thought, when he had gotten home. *I'll get in one more ride before I have to call it quits for this bike riding season.*

With only a flashing tail light set on random flash for safety (he eschewed a head lamp) he made his way along the streets that led out of town, letting the street lights guide him. He always rode with traffic and was alert to any oncoming vehicles, especially at intersections. But, cutting through the cemetery, he avoided two busy intersections and a busy street between them. So he had taken the graveyard shortcut on the way out of town, and now again on his way back approaching the end of his brisk, 20-mile ride. The cemetery was dark, but he knew the roads were well maintained and free from major potholes. Nonetheless, his eyes scoured the road in front of him for any hazards which may have fallen across the path since he had passed going the opposite direction almost an hour and a half ago.

He should have been home by now, but a flat tire had surprised him halfway through his ride. He usually carried a spare tube with him, but had given it to a fellow rider last Saturday morning on a group ride. That rider had had a flat and did not have a tube with him. Being a good friend meant letting the man have a tube. Bob had just forgotten to replace it when he had returned home. He had cursed when he discovered the omission.

He did have a patch kit with him, but patching a tube took more time than putting on a new one. After he had gotten the tire off and the old tube out, he did an inspection of the inside of the tire to see if he could find the item which had given him the problem. If the cause of the flat was not determined, and the foreign object remained, the repaired tube could go flat again.

"There you are, you little bastard," he had said aloud. "A little damn piece of glass."

He had carefully marked the way the tire had come off the bike so that he could put it back on in the same position. The tube would be aligned by the valve stem and the puncture point inside the tube. Putting the tube inside the tire in this manner would ensure that the hole left by the removed piece of glass would be aligned with the tube patch providing protection for the tube from any debris entering the hole. Just to be safe, however, he had decided to put a boot, another patch, on the tire itself. Pocketing the piece of glass (he didn't want to ride over it again the next time he rode this route) he then put the repaired wheel back on the bike.

Ordinarily he could replace a flat in ten to fifteen minutes, but patching the tube and booting the tire had taken an extra ten. The twenty-five added minutes, would keep him out past dark.

He raced back toward town cursing because he had also forgotten his cell phone. Otherwise, he could have called his wife had the darkness made it too dangerous to ride.

"Damn!" he said aloud as he lay on the ground. "Damn me for forgetting to take the cell phone."

His attempts to stand with a knee that hurt worse than his wrists (which had knife blades of pain shooting through them) left him in severe agony. Reaching down to touch his knee produced a handful of warm liquid which could only be blood, although it was too dark to see if it was or not. Groping in the dark for his bike, he found it and pulled it closer to see if he could use it as a crutch and maybe, somehow, get back on it and at least use his good leg to get himself home. He found the handlebar and dragged it closer.

What he found horrified him. His expensive carbon-fiber handlebar was snapped off close to where it had been connected to the bike. He had paid $260 last winter for the ultra-light-weight, shock absorbing, FSA, K-force bars. Now they were useless. Even if he were able to get back on the bike there was no way to ride it three feet let alone the three more miles to his home. Steering would be difficult and with his bad wrists, he couldn't hold the broken piece and use the rear brakes at the same time. Still lying on his back, he yanked his helmet off and removed his biking shoes, tossing them beside the bike.

After a lot of pain and effort, he was able to sit up and look around. The nearest traveled road was about five-hundred feet away. The street light on that road came on and as it warmed up it cast a little light in his direction, but, just as it got to maximum illumination, it blinked out.

Short cycling, he thought, remember what his electrical engineer friend called it. He closed his eyes, half in frustration and half in grimace, against the intense pain shooting through his wrists and knee. When he opened them again, the light was back on and growing brighter.

Just what I need, he thought. *A malfunctioning streetlight to add to my problems.*

When the light got to it's brightest, he looked to see what had brought him so quickly to the ground.

It must be a huge pothole, he thought. *One big enough to swallow my front wheel flipping me forward causing me to break my fall with my wrists and right knee.*

And those damn handlebars, he added.

But the only hole nearby was an eight-inch dip in the road with a metal plate at the bottom with the word "water" cast into it.

"Son of a bitch!" Bob cried out in disbelief. "I can't believe that a water shut-off valve access hole did it."

But it had.

The pain was getting worse as swelling around his one knee and both wrists put pressure on the joints. He tried to stand again, but couldn't bear any weight on his bad knee. With his hands, he tried to right the bike in an attempt to use it as a crutch on which he could support the bad side of his body and use his good leg to hobble over to the road. As he grabbed hold of the bike, he realized this, too, would not work since the pain in his wrists was as bad, or worse than his knee.

I'll crawl if I have to, he thought. But that, too, proved futile as he could not drag himself with his hands. He tried to get on his elbows and one good knee and did make it about ten feet before collapsing in pain.

"Damn, I'm going to lie here all night," he said aloud.

There was a flash of light from the direction of the street. Thinking that a car might be coming, he looked up in that direction, but saw no cars. Then he understood what the flash was as the sound of distant thunder filled the air. A front was approaching from the west, from the same direction as the malfunctioning street light. He thought about yelling, but that would only work if someone was within earshot. The only movement he saw in the direction of the street was an occasional car going too fast and making too much noise for the driver to hear him. With the storm approaching, no one would be out taking a walk or poop-walking their dog and it was getting later by the minute.

What time is it? he wondered. He did not have on a watch since bike computers, along with speed, average speed, time traveled, and mileage also displayed the time. His was an even fancier computer which gave him grades and elevations which told him why he was breathing and sweating so hard when going up a steep hill.

Another flash of lightning distracted him from finding out what time it was.

"One thousand one, one thousand two, one thousand three," he counted aloud.

He had gotten to four when the clap of thunder reached him telling him that the storm was less than a mile away. He remembered this little tool from his childhood and found out later in science class that the speed of sound in air was about 1125 feet per second. Therefore, five seconds of travel equaled about one mile. No matter what, the storm was almost on him.

The wind was picking up and another flash of lightning with the sound coming in two seconds meant that he was going to get drenched in addition to his present problems. Yelling for help now would really be futile. He felt a few drops of rain on the side of his head and he could hear the rain hitting the pavement toward the west. A clap of thunder immediately followed another flash of lightning.

Jesus, he thought. *I could be hit by lightning too.*

He thought of his wife, and whether or not she would panic when she got home and found him gone. He often walked to work, so his car being there without him would not be that unusual. And, with both of them working and keeping odd hours, they often would not eat together. They opted instead for separate meals at separate times and going to separate rooms to watch their favorite shows on separate TVs.

Married, but separate, he thought. *She might not even think of looking to see if my bike was missing from the garage.*

So, she might not even miss him until eight or nine o'clock, or later if she fell asleep in front of the TV. As the rain started coming in sheets on the blowing west wind, in a quest to find the computer with its time of day readout he dragged himself toward the bike using his forearms and good knee. When he got to the bike, he found that he could not read the computer in the dark. He pulled it off the broken handle bars and held it so that it would catch light from the next lightning strike.

When a bolt illuminated the sky, he saw that it was eight o'clock.

Thank God the lightning is cloud to cloud, instead of cloud to ground, he thought. *My chances of getting hit are less.*

He also remembered from his childhood the warnings to get to a low-lying area when caught outside in a lightning storm. *Well, that is not possible this time*, he thought. *The only low-lying areas around me are already occupied by the cemetery inhabitants.*

Still on his forearms and good knee, he looked up from the computer and caught a glimpse of movement to his right. Or at least he thought it was movement.

Just probably sheets of rain, he thought, *but maybe....*

"Hello," he called out. "Someone there?"

No answer.

"Humph! Who in their right mind would be out in this storm?" he said aloud.

Another movement made him look to his left.

"Oh, Jesus!"

What he saw was ghoulish, or appeared that way in the brief flash from a lightning bolt. It reminded him of that low-budget, black and white, late 1960's movie, *Night of the Living Dead*, a particularly gory depiction of zombies feasting on the poor souls of one little town.

Not sure what he had seen, if anything, he lay very still with his head constantly turning. Remembering that he had once used his tire pump to chase away a persistent country dog (usually one yell was enough to send them home), and without looking in the bike's direction he groped for the down tube behind the front wheel where the pump was stored. His hands hit pay dirt and he yanked the pump from its mounting hardware. It wasn't much of a weapon, but it was all he had.

Thank God it hadn't fallen off the bike when I fell, he thought.

"Ahhhh!" he screamed, as a tug on his bad leg sent a wave of excruciating pain throughout his body starting in his injured knee.

Another tug on his swollen left wrist caused him to drop the pump that he had held in his right hand.

Gale-force rain pummeled his body and lightning flashed all around. A deafening din of thunder muffled more of his screams as other forces tugged at his hair and other leg. Just as the old torture of tying a man's limbs to four separate horses and then having the horses yank simultaneously, he was being drawn and quartered.

The storm continued to rage and the rains continued as his screams ceased. The blood was soon washed away in torrents of water from the skies. After an hour, the storm passed by and the only trace of Bob were a busted up bike, a pair of shoes, and a helmet lying on a path in an old cemetery. Although the search had begun that night when his wife reported him missing, the bike, helmet, and shoes were not found until the next morning by a cemetery worker.

No one found out what had really happened that night. It was assumed that Bob had taken a nasty spill, had tried to walk home in an injured and perhaps delirious state, and had fallen into the nearby tributary which fed the Mahoning River north of town.

"He musta drowned and got swept away," his fellow bikers said. "He died doing what he liked best."

While installing an underground irrigation system fifteen years later, an unmarked grave was discovered beneath the path where Bob's last ride had ended. Six bodies were discovered, one in scattered pieces. The bodies were given a cursory, mandatory investigation, placed in caskets, and relocated to a back lot away from the other graves which had markers. A plain stone was set with "unknowns" cut into it. With the remains of the six bodies were pieces of clothing. In addition to normal street clothes, there was one pair of shorts, a three-pocket bicyclist's shirt, and a pair of fingerless gloves. Although the workers and investigators thought that the last items did not seem to fit in with the other clothes, none of them were cyclists and since fifteen-years had gone by, none of them could have suspected that Bob had worn them on his last ride.

The Loyal Order
Of The
Brotherhood Of The Butt

Allow me to start this story at the beginning and finish it at the end, the beginning and end of the digestive system that is. Get it? Huh? Huh? Get it?

The Beginning

I really don't mind going to the dentist, in fact I look forward to it. This is almost entirely because of a dentist that I had in Texas. As well as all the functions that a dentist performs, she did her own cleaning, which meant that she spent more time with the patient. While she was looking down at my mouth, I was looking up at her sparkling blue eyes and long blond hair. Since she wore a face mask I couldn't see much of anything else.

Enthralled, hypnotized, and numbed are about as descriptive as I can get in conveying how I felt as I lay back in the dentist chair, letting her do anything she wanted. She would always ask me what I had been doing and I responded as best I could with instruments or cleaning devices in my mouth. Noticing that I had listed a colonoscopy on the patient data under "Recent Surgeries," she asked me who did it and how it went. I wasn't sure whether a colonoscopy (this had been my third) was classified as surgery, but I listed it anyway.

"I just had one, too," she said, and then added. "I went through the procedure without any anesthesia."

"Really?" I questioned, only it came out like "rar-ry" as she poked around in my mouth.

"Yes," she replied, without any bragging in her voice. "It really didn't hurt that much, and I was able to help ease the scope around the bends in the colon by pushing on my abdomen with my hands."

Dang, I thought.

I had been told that a colonoscopy was extremely painful and all patients were put to sleep.

Could she be lying? I wasn't sure, but one look into those eyes told me she was being truthful. If a beautiful, petite, and fragile looking woman could go without anesthesia, then I could, by God, and from that day forward, I vowed to undergo my next colonoscopy without being put under. Since nothing that wasn't supposed to be there had been discovered during my last procedure, I would have to wait ten more years to test my bravado.

Ten years later I had my appointment. The day before the procedure, I was having "Breakfast with the Biker Boys," a small group of bicyclists who get together for breakfast in the winter when we can't ride outside together.

"I'm ordering only coffee," I said. "I'm prepping for a colonoscopy and can't eat today or tomorrow morning."

Sympathetic "ahhs" came from all those who had had one already. This included everyone seated since, at sixty-four, I was the youngest one there. My brother-in-law (BiL), John, was seated across from me and had undergone the procedure just a couple of months before.

I had gone to pick him up in the outpatient area just after he had come out of the procedure room.

The nurse had been coming in and out while I was there shouting "John! John! Wake up." She was not having much success as he never stirred from the drug-induced sleep and her interruptions were disturbing my efforts to read the local newspaper.

"I know what will wake him up," I said, after her third effort.

She gave me a sideways glance and a who-do-you-think-you-are sneer. I ignored her disdainful look and said one word.

"Handel's," I said, in a normal tone of voice, turning my eyes back to the paper that I had been reading.

"Handel's?" came the raspy reply. "We gonna get Handel's?"

"Yeah," I said. "As soon as we get outta here."

Handel's is a locally owned ice cream booth that has, if not the best ice cream in the area, at least the best in our town. John loves Handel's, and I knew it. Besides, having not eaten for a day and a half, some Handel's ice cream would taste mighty good.

Because I had succeeded where she had failed, the nurse gave me an even dirtier look than she had given me earlier.

"He likes Handel's," I responded, as she stomped out of the cubicle.

So there was my BiL sitting across from me when I announced that I was only allowed to have coffee for breakfast.

"And, he's going to do it without anesthesia," he added to my pronouncement.

"What?" the others responded. "Are you nuts?"

"I did it that way," Mel added.

Mel, coincidentally another dentist albeit retired, had seen painful situations, and knows when anesthesia is really needed.

"There wasn't anything to it," he said, matter-of-factly with a so-what look. "It was easy."

That cemented my resolve. *By God, I'm gettin' it without being put to sleep*, I thought.

The others just shook their heads and we moved on to another topic of discussion, how to solve the musty/dirty smell and taste of the city water.

The next day I had my BiL take me to the outpatient clinic where the procedure was to be done. After checking in, I was led to my cubical and told to strip down to my socks.

What's with the socks, I thought.

I lay in the bed awaiting my turn with the long black snake-like probe, in an open-in-the-back hospital gown, with my socks the only protection between me and the outside world.

"What's your birthday?" the day nurse asked for the umpteenth time.

"What? Are you, planning a surprise birthday party for me?" I asked. "Everybody keeps asking me my birthdate."

"We'll have the doctor and the anesthesiologist comes in next to brief you on the procedure" she said, with not so much as a smile.

"I'm not getting put to sleep," I responded.

"You don't want any anesthetic?" she asked incredulously.

"Nope," I said unconvincingly, with maybe a little quaver in my voice. "If I can just get a happy pill, I'll be satisfied."

I remembered that last time that I had gone through this, I had been given a pill that made me not care what happened next. I called it a happy pill for lack of any other identification.

"I don't have a happy pill," she said, just barely raising her eyes off the clipboard full of papers in front of her. "Are you sure you don't want any drugs?"

"Positive," I said, this time not so sure.

"I'll have the doctor talk to you about no anesthetic," she added. "We'll put in an IV just in case."

In case you wuss out, was the thoughtful look on her face.

"Okay," I said.

Five minutes later the doctor came in. He was the only one who did not ask me my birthdate. This was probably because he had been a member of the bike riding club that I had had breakfast with the day before. He quit riding after his second crash, the one where a dog ran out in front of him, causing him to do an ENDO (up over the handle bars). He hit his head on the pavement and cracked his helmet right after "T-boning" the canine.

"I can't risk getting injured and not being able to provide for my family," was how I think he put it when he had announced that he wouldn't ride anymore. It's hard to be a one-armed proctologist.

"So, you want to do this without any anesthetic?" Dr. Park asked, as he closed the curtain to the cubicle behind him.

"Yeah," I said. "I'd like to try it. What kind of pain can I expect?"

"Severe cramping," he said.

"How many have gone without being put to sleep?" I asked, and then added. "I hate being put to sleep. The recovery is so much longer. If I'm in too much pain, can you put me to sleep during the procedure?"

"I've known five or six to do without," he said. "I can administer an anesthetic, but what I use has a longer recovery time than what the anesthesiologist uses."

I hesitated, and then thought about the petite dentist who did this. *If she can do it, and Mel said that 'it was so easy', then I can do it.*

"Let's do it without." I said, still trying to convince myself. "My only concern is pain when you insert the probe. I was told that I had had a lot of pain the first time I had this done, but I don't remember it."

"I'll use extra lubricant," he assured me.

He left me alone to ponder my decision. A few minutes later, he came back.

"Will you help me with a practical joke that I want to play on the nurses?" he asked. "It's April Fools Day and I always get the two same nurses."

"Sure," I said. "What do you want me to do?"

"Pretend like you can't go through the procedure with them in the room," he went on. "Say something like they 'bother' you."

"Okay," I added.

He left and I planned what I would say once I got in the procedure room.

"Are you ready?" a nurse said as she pulled the curtain aside. She was dressed in a gown and must be one of the two nurses the doc had been talking about.

"Sure," I said, not wanting to start my spiel until we got to the room.

"You are requesting no anesthesia?" she said, incredulously as she pushed me and the bed down the corridor.

"I sure am," I said, this time convinced that I could this.

"Hi Doc," I said cheerfully as we entered the procedure room.

He was the only other person in the room that was practically wall-to-wall equipment. As I was admiring all the neat stuff and getting a lay for the room, Nurse Two walked in and started to put on a gown.

"Hi," she said cheerfully, after she got her gown on. "What's your birthdate?"

Just to see what would happen, I was tempted to give her the wrong date, but blurted out the correct date instead.

"Man, there are some bad vibes in this room," I said, eliciting no response.

"Oh, it's coming from you," I added, with a nod to the nurse who had just come in. "You're making me feel uncomfortable." Again, silence.

"You too," I said, turning toward Nurse One who had just brought me in. "I don't think I can do this with you two in the room. I need another set of nurses."

They still said nothing, but both looked toward the doc with concern on their faces. I glanced at the doc, and he was also displaying a look of 'what do you want me to do about it' on his face.

"Doc," I continued, "you're either going to have to tell them to leave, or…tell them what day this."

"April Fool!" Nurse Two blurted out, as she realized what day it was.

Relieved laughter followed from Nurse One who was out of sight behind me. Doc Park didn't have to say anything, but I saw a big smile on his face.

"You get me every year," Nurse Two said, with a smile. "You really had me going."

The latter comment was directed to me.

"You're a good actor," Doc Park said.

"Well, I'm a writer," I said in response.

"So, you're going to do this without any anesthesia?" Nurse Two asked.

"Yeah," I said. "I want to make sure doc doesn't have both hands on my shoulders."

It was an old joke, and got the same response that old jokes that have been heard before get. The subdued snickers were the same as when I had told the dentist that he was looking down in the mouth today.

The fun was over, and now it was on to the business at hand – rather, further down the anatomy.

I rolled over onto my left side as I was instructed to do, at which time my attention turned to the large color monitor just above my head. Frankly, I don't ever remember seeing my butt before with such clarity as the probe approached its destination. I've never even thought of using a mirror to get a look. Now I knew why.

The pain I had dreaded as the procedure started never materialized. I was much relieved.

This is going to be easy, I thought.

"How ya doin'?" Doc said.

"Fine," I replied, followed by a "What's that?"

There were a lot of what's thats during the procedure followed by some explanation from the doc. It was all new to me, but Doc was familiar with a lot of the assholes in our city, so nothing surprised him. I was fascinated by this journey through the human body – my body. The probe was approaching the first big bend going from left to right across my abdomen.

"You'll feel a little cramping here," Doc said.

When he hit the bend, I hit the ceiling. Well, almost. It was as he had described, there was some severe cramping as the probe tried to straighten out the intestine. I grabbed hold of the metal guardrail on the side of the bed and squeezed.

"Take in a deep breath," Nurse One said from behind me, as the skin on my knuckles turned as white as copy paper.

The pain could only be described as what I would have felt if I had eaten El Grande Bean Burrito at Don Pancho's Tex-Mex Cafe an hour before and it was building up El Grande load of gas.

I took a quick deep breath, but exhaled as fast as I had taken it in.

"Help it around the bend," Doc said.

Nurse Two who was now sitting on a stool near my knees put some pressure on my stomach to massage the probe around the ninety-degree turn.

"Let the breath out slowly," Nurse One said.

I tried to obey, but before I could get it right, the pain was gone.

"Are you okay?" Doc said.

"Sure," I replied, with eyes wide and a death grip on the rail. "Can I have a bullet to bite on?"

"We don't have any bullets," Nurse Two said.

"See that dark spot?" Doc asked. "That's your liver up against the intestine wall. The colon wall is very thin, but strong."

"Yeah! Wow!" I said, as he moved the camera back out so that I could see it better.

"The second turn is coming up," Doc warned.

"Breathe deeply and let it out slowly," both nurses said in unison.

Another death grip on the hand rail and I realized that they were trying to get me to do the controlled breathing part of the Lamaze method for delivering a baby without drugs. This time, with their coaxing, I obeyed. The second bend to my relief was not as bad as the first.

"We're at the cecum, the beginning of the colon," Doc informed. "You can see some villi at the end of the small intestine and there's your appendix."

The villi are the tiny protrusions that do all the nutrient absorption in the small intestine and, of course, my appendix was still intact and serving no purpose.

"You must not have had an appendectomy," Nurse One said.

Brilliant observation, I thought, but was too amazed at the images on the screen to add that zinger to the April Fool's joke.

"There's a polyp," Doc said, "and another one."

He sounded a little bit like John Huston had when he had found gold in the 1948 movie *Treasure of the Sierra Madres*. I half expected him to do a little jig.

"Put the patch on him," Doc told Nurse One.

"You're going to feel something cold," she said, as she pealed off the protective layer from the adhesive portion of what must have been a large bandage.

A freezer was probably where it had been stored before she laid it on my exposed side. The shock was almost as bad as the probe going around the first bend.

"I get a better look as I back out," Doc informed me.

My eyes were glued to the screen.

"See the polyp?" Doc asked.

It was difficult to see and I had expected some large, ominous looking growth frowning down at me. Instead what I saw was a whitish, pink bump on the intestinal wall, hardly noticeable to the untrained eye.

I've had pimples bigger than that, I thought.

Then I saw something amazing. As I watched, a metal tube reached out and from its end, four little fingers jumped up and like a cat grabbing a mouse, closed around the unsuspecting polyp. As I watched, spellbound, my right leg jumped a couple of times.

"Did you feel that?" Doc asked, as the fingers retracted and the little pink piece of intestine disappeared from the end of the tube.

"No," I said. "My leg just jumped uncontrollably."

"Oh," Doc said, noticing my death grip. "Take your hands off the guardrail."

"That's a cauterizing tool, too?" I asked, as I realized that a portion of the electricity meant for the end of the tool, made its way to the metal guardrail via my right leg.

"That's a grounding strap on my side," I added to my rhetorical question, my electrical engineer training kicking in. "And I just grounded myself through the guardrail."

"Yes," Doc said, while the tool grabbed the second polyp and it, too, disappeared.

"Oh, and that little tool also has a vacuum on it," I observed. "Did ya get it?"

"Yes," he said. "We got it."

"I gotta get me one of those." I said, knowing that that little tool probably cost more than my truck had when it was new.

As he backed slowly out of the intestine, no other polyps were found. At the end of the colon, Doc turned the camera tube back on itself to see if anything was in the rectum, the last six to eight inches of the colon.

Then the procedure was over.

"Except for the first bend, that wasn't so bad," I exclaimed, proud that I had now joined the "Brotherhood of the Butt," those who have had a colonoscopy without anesthesia (this also includes women). I had known of two before my procedure, me, and with the five or six Doc knew of, there are at least eight of us now in the club.

"You did very well," Doc said as he snapped off his latex gloves. "Call me next week for your biopsy results."

"Yes," Nurse Two echoed. "After as well as you did, I'm going to tell the other patients that they don't need anesthesia."

The End

Get it? Huh? Huh? Get it?

Epilog

The best part of the anesthesia-free procedure is that there is no recovery period afterwards. When I got back to my room, got dressed, and signed the post-op papers, I was on my way out. As far as the pain – not knowing what to expect was worse than actually experiencing it. Now that I know, you can bet my next colonoscopy will again be without anesthesia. If you want to join the Brotherhood, talk with your doctor. You will experience a lot worse sources of pain then that of a colonoscopy and the reward of seeing the procedure on a monitor is well worth it. Remember, deep breaths and slow exhales.

I called Doc a week later and he said that my polyps were benign. When I mentioned my procedure to a group of high school classmates, over (of all things) lunch, I found another female member of the Brotherhood.

Every year, Doc Park has an oriental food booth at the "Guys Who Can Cook" festival at the church fund-raiser. I think if he has Polynesian Polyps on the menu, I'll eat something else.

PART THREE

She's the Best
&
I Dropped My Rocks In Siberia

I thought I was really in trouble the day I dropped my rocks in the limnological museum near Lake Baikal in Siberia, just as the Cold War was starting to thaw. That single event could have set back détente by ten years.

Let me first explain limnological museums and Lake Baikal. Limnological, to me and most people back then, had never heard the term before. Limnology means the scientific study of the life and phenomena of fresh water, especially lakes and ponds. Museums in Russia means churches, which, after the "Glorious October Revolution of 1908," were no longer needed for worship and were converted to museums. But instead of God, the converted churches were for the worship of Lenin and the glorious heroes of the October Revolution that ousted the czars and put the Bolsheviks in power. This was all explained by Gunter, our Russian guide who was a KGB agent assigned to make sure freedom loving Americans saw whatever they wanted to see, as long as it was the lake museum, Lenin's tomb, or a bauxite plant.

Gunter's most used line was "it is forbidden," followed by a list of things we could not do, such as selling our Levis for $90 a pair, or taking rubles out of Mother Russia, or bringing *Playboy* magazines into the country. He never did tell us what the penalties would be if we did the forbidden, but I really did not want to find out. Every day there was a new list of forbiddens, usually after one of us did a forbidden thing, so we were always kept on edge. We soon realized that the it-is-forbidden warning meant "don't do it again."

Gunter also made sure freedom loving Russians were kept away from American tourists. If a local approached us, one look and some mumbled Russian from Gunter sent them scurrying away, blending easily back into the Russian populace who all wore the same dark-gray, mothball-scented overcoats; wool caps with ear flaps; black faux leather shoes; and gray scarves around their necks. And this was in July.

Lake Baikal, is in Siberia near the Mongolian border. The lake is conveniently located in the direction of travel across Siberia from east to west. Since none of their commercial planes could have flown nonstop very far without running out of fuel or losing a wing, a necessary stop was made in nearby Irkutsk. Lake Baikal is now commercialized and is a favorite tourist destination, but in 1978, few of us had ever heard of it.

With twenty percent of the earth's fresh water, Lake Baikal is the deepest fresh-water lake in the world and contains more water than all of the five Great Lakes combined. It's 1,620 meters deep, slightly over a mile, and sometimes freezes solid in the Siberian winter. So, now you know more than you wanted to about one of Siberia's fantastic attractions, and probably more than the average Russian did back during the Cold War.

Our trip to the lake had started two days before on a sour note. We were airlifted from Khabarovsk to Irkutsk aboard an Aeroflot version of a DC10 which looked like a barn with wings. The seats, held down with leather straps to a wooden deck, were lawn chairs through which was telegraphed the impression of the backbone of the person seated in front of you. The meal served on this commuter flight consisted of undercooked seagull legs; dark-brown, dense, Russian bread; and frozen peas. The people in our tour group were the only passengers to get meals. The Russian passengers did not. I offered one of my seagull legs to the man in the wet, dark-gray, mothball-scented overcoat sitting in the lawn chair next to me, but he refused it. Obviously a frequent flyer on Aeroflot who had tasted the fare before, he did not even need a dirty look from Gunter to bypass the offering.

Let me explain why my frequent-flyer friend's coat was wet.

Awakening at 2:30 in the morning and leaving our hotel in Khabarovsk we hurried to the airport where we had a two-hour wait for our flight. To get on the plane, we were bused from our well lighted, warm, enclosed waiting area. As we were getting on the bus beneath a sheltered canopy, we saw a group of people leave a not very well lighted, dingy looking terminal and run the quarter mile toward the same plane we were to board. An airline official stopped the running hoard on the tarmac before they reached the stairs leading up to the plane. They were delayed until our buses arrived so that we could board first. The fact that it was pouring rain and dark was of no concern to the official.

As we climbed the stairs, past the pregnant woman holding a baby and past her rain soaked comrades, we held our heads high, proud to be Americans worthy of special treatment. Okay, we did slither on board like snakes crawling into a hole to escape the cold rainy night. I have never felt so low in all my life. When I apologized to my frequent-flyer friend about their having to wait, he said very proudly in broken English, "You are guests in my country." Gunter smiled broadly at the canned response.

After running into a flock of seagulls near the airport, we landed in Irkutsk. As we were deplaning past the same pregnant woman and her still drenched baby, I noticed a cart of dead seagulls being wheeled toward the terminal. No doubt, they would be prepared for the next group of tourists on their way to Irkutsk, or for our continuing flight in a couple of days to Moscow to visit Lenin's tomb, where I almost got shot – another story.

A bus took us to our hotel which was supposed to be a nice Intourist hotel, but when we arrived, that hotel was full. Staying there was a Smithsonian tour group who themselves looked like traveling exhibits; therefore, we were rerouted to a "nice" Russian hotel.

The Hotel Siberia (the real name) was the pits! It was dingy, smelly, dirty, roach-infested, dilapidated, and unheated – those were the nice parts of it. The showers were down the hall but we did have a dirty toilet with a seat made from pressed fiberboard. Getting splinters in the butt was minor when faced with using the toilet paper which was akin to the paper hand towels we had had in our public schools back in the fifties. Pieces of bark and chunks of wood were visible in the dark color of the tissue. To call it tissue was using one's imagination. We had been cautioned to bring toilet paper with us, but we hadn't and up until now, had not had to. But in this "hotel" we faced the real possibility of removing skin while cleansing ourselves. The sink was useable, but had the markings of the thousands of Ivans and Natashas who had preceded us. The showers down the hall were shared with the other guests on our floor.

Since we had gained two hours passing through time zones, it was only 7:30 local time when we arrived. Breakfast, which would really be lunch for us, was not until 9:00; therefore, we had time to kill. Sally and I walked to a nearby park where we just sat and watched the typical Siberian people on their way to work. I'm not a stylish maven, but even I noticed that the women wore mismatched and terribly out-dated clothes. They all had the same reddish-orange hair and heavy, blue eye shadow. The men wore the dark-gray obligatory wool, mothball-saturated overcoats with matching pants. On their heads were the Stalin-era fur caps. We weren't close enough to smell mothballs, but behind everyone who passed by, small insects were dropping from the air like firecracker ash on the Fourth of July.

Back at the hotel, breakfast was the same as we had had every morning and would have every morning on the rest of our three-week tour. Awaiting us were eggs; a hard, salami-like sausage; unsalted brown bread; unsalted butter; and tea. Sally's idea of breakfast is toast, so I got to eat her portion too. As with the toilet paper we were also told to bring peanut butter and powdered Tang. Again, wishing to pack light, we hadn't, but others had, which was a saving grace. A week into the trip, because of the lack of fresh fruits and vegetables (with the exception of cucumbers), some of us were developing scurvy, which was cured with the vitamin C in Tang.

As was typical for our Russian trip, after breakfast we boarded a bus for a tour of the city and our trip to the Taiga. Our tour to Lake Baikal would occur tomorrow. Pulling away from the hotel, we saw our luggage being off loaded from an open truck. It was soaking wet! Aeroflot had not protected the baggage on the tarmac when we had left Khabarovsk in the pouring rain.

The trip into a forest like region was mostly on hard packed, dirt and gravel roads with no other traffic and lots of vegetation, mainly trees. There was one stop along the way at a spring where we drank the water cascading directly down the side of a hill. I assumed that there were no animals upstream as the water was clean, clear, and delicious. It certainly tasted better than the terrible tasting bottled water (affectionately called lolli-water) available to us. The bottled water was ordained lolli-water by our tour director Paul Gazelle. He had likened it to water that had had a lollipop dipped into it to give it flavor. One taste of it and you realized why Russians preferred to drink vodka.

Since we were going for a luncheon picnic in the Taiga, the talk centered on the food and all were hoping for hotdogs and hamburgers. An hour later, we arrived at a log cabin in a little clearing surrounded by large trees.

Since no one lived in the forest, our hosts for the meal and all the food had been brought on the bus with us. The preparers needed time to get the meal ready so our KGB guide, Gunter, announced that we would go for a "little walk." This was a forest after all, so the little walk actually consisted of mountain climbing for which no one had prepared in the way of clothing or shoes. Forty-five minutes later we trekked back to the cottage for the picnic.

Intourist had provided ten bottles each of Russian vodka (more like a strong wine) and Champagne (more like a weak brandy) and since we had a little rest period before lunch was served, we opened the bottles and started passing them around. There was some lolli-water, but because we had all tasted the bottled water before, we opted for the vodka and Champagne. After we had gotten quite lubricated, we were ushered inside the cabin to begin our picnic.

One of the unattached men on the tour became enamored with our young, pretty waitress, Vera, who had ridden on the bus with us and who would accompany us on the way back. She spoke no English, and he spoke no Russian, but someone had handed him an English-Russian dictionary. When she wasn't serving food and for the entire ride back on the bus, they spent their time pointing to words in the book.

We were pleasantly surprised that instead of American fare we had sausage; a salad of onions, cabbage, peas, and yogurt; and, of course, the Russian brown bread. I particularly liked the salad which had as a garnish, garlic chives, something I had never had before. The alcohol was almost all gone when they brought out even more food. This time it was beef patties, macaroni, and bran muffins. Then, typical for Russian meals, the toasts started with what little alcohol was left. Heidi and Gale, who had met when he was her teacher in an American high school in Japan, sat next to us. They had celebrated their three-year wedding anniversary just the day before.

As the salutes went around, we were all getting even tipsier.

When it got to be their turn, Gale lifted his glass and said in a muffled voice, "To Heidi, she's the best fuck in the place."

One of the two older women, who were traveling together, turned to her companion and, so that she could be heard above the laughter, asked in a squeaky loud voice, "What did he say?"

To which her friend answered in an equally loud response, "He said, that she is the best fuck in the place."

This brought even more howls of laughter from the rest of us and set the tone for the ride back.

Arriving back at the hotel at 5:30, I wanted to get cleaned up. After all, we had been up since 12:30 AM local time, had flown on a smelly plane, had taken five bus rides, had hiked in the Russian forest, and had gotten plastered, all in the same clothes.

As I said, the shower was down the hall. When I approached the shower area it was guarded by a Babushka who handed out towels like a matron in a fancy hotel lobby restroom. From her gesturing and tone of voice I understood that the showers were full. I shrugged and went back to the room to wait fifteen minutes. Another trip down the hall resulted in the same response. Sally and I decided to take a nap before dinner, only to sleep all the way past the dinner hour.

After the nap, I tried again three more times, and on the final try, I had noticed a woman coming in from the street and handing the guard some rubles for which she received a towel and admittance to the shower stall. Frustrated, I gave up until the next morning when I found no Babushka, just a stack of towels. Apparently Russians don't take morning showers and she was renting shower stalls at night to the entire town of Irkutsk.

After breakfast and the same old eggs, salami, and unsalted brown bread and butter, we boarded the tour bus for our trip to Lake Baikal. It happened to be election day and the polling places were jammed with voters. That's a lie. There were no voters in sight, but Gunter assured us that everyone voted. The next day he proclaimed that the Communist Party had received ninety-eight percent of the votes. When asked about the other two percent, he stated that they were marked incorrectly and had to be tossed out. Of course we believed him. Russian democracy in action! What a country!

The bus trip to Lake Baikal took an hour and a half, passing by many collective lumber yards. The rainy morning gave way to a sunny day, but the temperature was still quite low for what we were used to in June at our starting point on tropical Okinawa. Our bus tour ended at the shores of the lake, and under the careful watch of Gunter, we were allowed to roam freely on the shoreline, which consisted of about fifty feet of gravel and rocks. There was a beach of sorts, if you like to lie on pebbles the size of golf balls and bask in the searing fifty-five degree heat of midday in June. Also, you could go swimming in the forty degree water if you liked to raise goose bumps. We all kept our coats on and our collars pulled up tightly against the balmy breeze blowing in off the lake.

Thinking that it would be durable and warm enough for June and July, I had only brought a denim jacket. Obviously the others had read the tour book and brought warmer clothing. In my defense, they had been living on mainland Japan or were from the States and had winter clothing. Living on Okinawa, all we had were clothes for weather which rarely went below fifty, even in the coldest part of winter.

Gunter told us that the lake water was pure and safe to drink. One of our members bent down to the water, cupped his hands, and took a drink. It was then that Gunter drew our attention to the sea lions out in the lake sunning themselves on rocks after they, no doubt, had had their morning defecation close to the shoreline. I think I heard the lake-water drinker gag a little bit.

I pointed to some more sea lions a short way down on the beach and asked Gunter why they were so close to people. Just then, one of them sat up and I noticed they were not sea lions, but Russian women wearing black, one-piece bathing suits proudly displaying their winter, protective layer of insulation while basking in the sun. Gunter gave me a dirty look which caused me to cringe a bit, but I was snickering inside.

To avoid his glare and hide my amusement, I bent down and examined some of the rocks, picking up some interesting specimens. I pocketed at least three for me and several others for those who had asked that I bring them back a souvenir of Russia.

"A rock will do," one of them had proclaimed.

Thinking that was a great and inexpensive gift solution, I filled my jacket pockets.

After a half hour of looking at water, rocks, and sea lions, Gunter announced, "We now go to the lunch and then the limnological museum."

Following Gunter back to the bus like lemmings toward a cliff, we were looking at each other wondering what a limnological museum was. Lunch had been at a very fine restaurant overlooking the lake where we were served batter-fried fish that had come from the lake. It might have been tasty, but all we could savor was the batter. Just as had happened before entering the restaurant, when we left, we were approached by children wanting chewing gum. Having read that part of the tour guide, Sally and I had plenty of gum to pass out.

Arriving at the church/museum, we were still wondering what the museum contained. It looked like a church with a beautiful stone exterior, but where we expected to see ornate windows there was only clear glass. What windows that weren't clear glass were covered over with stone-like material to hide any religious designs.

We de-bused and piled inside to what used to be the narthex of a Russian Orthodox Church. The inside was beautiful, but all of the religious items had been removed or covered up. The floor was marble, and the inside walls were all gray stone. Large wooden doors led in from outside and through the narthex and into the nave. We never got to see the rest of the church, because all of the museum pieces were in the narthex.

One of the braver guys from our group, I think it was the lake drinker, asked what a limnological museum was.

Gunter looked at us in disgust, and pointed to a plastic cross-section of Lake Baikal in the middle of the room and said, "It is dedicated to the lake."

We all stared at the model as Gunter continued with his spiel about its depth, length, girth, and volume, all in metric, so we had no idea how big it was. Against the walls were models of small boats, pictures of animals that inhabited the area, maps, and other boring stuff all depicting how in awe we should have been to be there. The pictures made it all look barren and cold.

By now, the sun was coming in through the large, clear windows and was warming the room. When we realized Gunter was not all the way through his story of the lake and how many rivers fed into it, a lot of us started taking off our jackets. Gunter had to name all the rivers and point to each on a large map tacked to the wall. Like the others had done, I took off my jacket forgetting about the cache of rocks in the pockets.

Just as Gunter said, "Lake Baikal is a natural treasure and it is forbidden to remove anything from the shoreline, even the rocks," I draped my jacket over my arm.

What happened next immediately froze the room. The only sound so far, had been Gunter talking with his voice echoing off the stone walls, ceiling, and floor of the enclosed room. As his "it is forbidden speech" was still reverberating off the walls, every rock in my collection tumbled out of the open pockets of my jacket. The noise as they hit the marble floor was deafening. It sounded like a coke bottle banging around in a metal trash can, and the clamor echoed off every hard surface in the room. Then there was complete silence.

All eyes were moving between me and Gunter, wondering what would happen next. My fellow travelers closest to me started to move quietly away, no doubt wanting to get out of the line of fire.

Not knowing what else to do, I calmly bent down and started picking up the rocks, proudly proclaiming, "My rock collection."

With my head lowered, trying to get the last rock that had rolled under the plastic model of the lake, I added, "I'd put them back, but I don't remember where they all go."

That must have broken the ice, for some in the crowd started to snicker, and Gale, my closest friend during the trip, had to go outside doubled up with laughter. Gunter never said a word about the dropped rocks, he just continued with his monologue about the lake. With my rocks back in my pocket, I joined Gale outside and we both burst out laughing. But for the rest of our tour in Irkutsk, I feared for my life.

On the way back, my rocks safely tucked in my pockets, we stopped and took pictures at a collective lumber yard, one of the many we had passed on the way to the lake. When we got back to the hotel we had forty-five minutes to kill before dinner at seven. Roaming around the hotel, I noticed the same routine with the Babushka and the showers.

After dinner, Heidi and Gale took a walk with us to the Angara River where we were stopped by several residents asking us if we spoke German. Apparently we at least did not look like Russians. We tried to make our way to a band concert on an island on the river, but were driven away by hoards of mosquitoes.

Music was coming from the dining room which was noisy and crowded. As was typical at most places, there was a doorman barring the way. Fresh from my episode at the museum I was afraid to make any moves involving a forced entry, but Sally was much bolder. He stepped aside as she pushed him out of the way. Russians seemed to respond passively to a show of force which we would use to our advantage throughout the trip.

I had used the bold approach more than once, but I remember one episode vividly. With the rest of the group at the Russian Circus in Moscow, we had made our way to the seats indicated on the ticket stub. When I had gotten to the corresponding row and seat number shown on my ticket, there was a Russian man sitting there. I tried to politely indicate that he was sitting in my seat. He started raving and I got the impression that under no circumstances was he going to move.

"Bull shitsky!" I shouted, thinking that he might understand a swearword if I had "Russianized" it.

I'm sure he did not know what the hell I was saying, but my tone and angry expression did the trick. He got up and walked away without saying another word.

After we had gained entry to the dining room, we noticed a lot of the people from our group sitting at a table. We joined them until midnight, sharing wine and vodka.

Gale and I went to bed while Heidi and Sally stayed up and talked until one-thirty in the morning in Heidi and Gale's room. When Sally headed to our room on a different floor, the elevator got stuck.

She tried to use the emergency phone, but could not make the Russian speaking person on the other end understand her plight. Being slightly claustrophobic, she started to panic and pounded on the doors until her hands stung. Fifteen Russian minutes later, the elevator responded and took her to our floor. She was nearly hysterical when she got to the room and, naturally, I tried to laugh it off.

The next morning we were up early and packed for the last leg of our trip in Mother Russia. After breakfast we bought some postcards, wrote on them, and mailed them off to the States. An attempted walk around Moscow was shortened by the rain, so we headed back to the hotel and chatted with some of the other tour members until lunch.

We said a tearful farewell (not) to It-is-forbidden Gunter who left us with another KGB tour guide who looked like Rosa Krebs from the James Bond movie *From Russia with Love*. As we boarded the bus for the train station, I half expected her to pop out a knife from the tip of her shoe and prod us onto the train for our next destination.

From Yak Belts to Coconuts

I tried to trade my passport for a yak belt, but he wanted my watch instead.

Let me explain.

Our trip from Moscow to what was originally St. Petersburg, renamed Leningrad, and now St. Petersburg once again, was by train. On our train trip across a portion of Siberia, Gale and I had seen enough of the Russian countryside, which was just trees and snow, and this was in July. It only got interesting when we got to a small town to put water in the steam engine. Then we could get off the train and buy the only food items available, which were boiled eggs, caviar, cucumbers and, of course, some vodka to wash it all down.

But now, on our way to St. Petersburg, the end of our cross-country Russian trip was coming to an end and we had been served enough hard-boiled eggs with caviar for breakfast to last us a long time. The salads for lunch and dinner had consisted of sliced cucumbers, period. There were no tomatoes, lettuce, or even carrots, just sliced cucumbers, so we had had our fill of cukes, too. Into our third week now, the powdered Tang was beginning to run out, and the scurvy we all had feared was becoming real. A couple of fellow travelers had experienced bleeding gums; however, when someone on our tour group had told us that there was vitamin C in vodka and brandy, Gale and I drank a few glasses every chance we got.

Train stops were also places to marvel at the modern machinery and housing construction. Actually, the bulldozers looked like pre-WWII equipment. Houses were almost all constructed of logs with two-foot wide spaces between the inner and outer windows for protection from freezing weather, which in Russia lasts from the beginning of August until the end of July. Summer was the first and second days of August.

The rest of the year was properly called winter. But anyway, I have digressed again and need to return to the story.

Gale and I dug the bottles of liquid vitamin C out of our hand-carry bags and looked for a place where we could drink our scurvy medicine in relative peace and privacy. Noise from the passengers was not a problem, since the seats on the train around where our group sat, were filled with girls on a Komosol field trip to either a bauxite plant or a memorial to the Glorious October Revolution. The Komosol was the Russian equivalent to the Girl Scouts, but instead of roasting marshmallows and selling cookies, there was a strict devotion to all things communistic, including marching and carrying rifles (I never asked if they were loaded or not). Their strict disciplinary regimen apparently also meant no smiling and no moving because they all sat on the train motionless and emotionless. With their hands clasped and kept at all times on the laps of their blue uniforms, they stared straight ahead trying to ignore the two Americans carrying bottles of vodka and brandy down the aisles toward the space between the cars.

As if it were our own private room, we commandeered the between-the-car space which I'm sure has a fancy name like loading/unloading deck. But, it was a place where we could be away from the watchful eyes of the Komosol girls and their babushka leaders. We opened our bottles and proceeded to protect ourselves from the ravages of bleeding gums while discussing what we would do when we got to Stalingrad. First on the list was to replenish our supply of scurvy medicine. So far, on our been-there-done-that list were, nearly getting me arrested at Lenin's tomb and being thrown out of the limnological museum. So we were anxious to see what adventures awaited us on the remainder of the trip.

Vodka and brandy sold in Russia is not all that strong. It has the alcohol content of wine, so that in one sitting, an entire bottle can be consumed without anyone dying. As we were imbibing, we approached a small town where the train started to slow. A short Russian man entered our space to de-train and obviously was trying to ignore us.

"Puzhalsta," I said, in a gesture of friendship offering him a drink from my bottle of brandy.

I believe the word puzhalsta (pronounced pajawlsta) means "here ya go," or something like that and was one of the few Russian words I knew. He took the bottle, and in true Russian fashion, took a drink, only it was a long pull. He almost finished the nearly-full bottle from which I had taken only a couple of sips.

"Spasiba," he said as the train came to a full stop.

I think the word means "thank you," or "damn Yankee bastard," or something close to that. With a toothless smile, he offered his hand and we shook.

"Puzhalsta," I said again.

In addition to "here ya go," I think puzhalsta also means "you're welcome," but could have meant "damn proud of it." The short Russian got off the train and the man who had just tried to ignore us moments ago turned and gave us a wave as the train got underway again. Ah, détente!

After Gale and I waved back, we looked at each other and shrugged. I held up my nearly empty bottle and said, "Oh well." I wasn't worried. I had another bottle in my hand-carry bag.

A man, who must have gotten on at the last stop, came into our little den from the same car we had come in from. There were no empty seats in that car since the Komosol girls and the others in our tour group, including our wives, had taken them all. So, I guessed that he may have been going to the next car to find a place to sit. His dungaree jacket, pants, and blue chambray shirt did not fit in with the normal Russian uniform of the day consisting of mothball-scented, dark-grey, wool overcoat and wool pants.

He hesitated just long enough so that Gale offered him a drink of vodka. He put down the bag he had slung over his shoulder and reached for the proffered bottle. I was not about to offer him any brandy because of how much our last Russian "friend" had drunk. The man seemed quite grateful and took a big swig, not a long pull, but a friendly drink.

"Thank you," he said in broken English.

"Puzhalsta," Gale said.

"I am Armenian," he said in a gruff voice, "not Rooskie."

"We are Americans," I chimed in.

"I know," he said proudly. "I have been to U.S.A. on ship." This confirmed my observation that some of his clothes looked like a nautical uniform.

I offered him some brandy and he took a drink.

"Nice belt," I said, pointing to the black fur-covered belt he proudly displayed. "What is it?" I said, trying to keep my words simple, so that he would understand.

"This yak," he said, pulling it out a little with his thumb for me to see. "From Tibet."

"Would you sell it to me?" I asked, as I offered him some more brandy.

"Mah-cha mon-yea," he said indicating it was expensive, but leaving the door open.

"Okay," I said, taking a drink from the bottle he had passed back to me.

"Wait," he said and bent to take something from the bag lying at his feet.

Gale and I stretched our necks to see what he was groping for. We were both surprised and impressed when he pulled a coconut from the bag.

"Coconut," he proudly proclaimed, holding his prize out for us to see. "We open."

I knew that coconuts were hard to open, so I expected him to pull a machete from his bag too, but knew he would never have gotten such a weapon through Russian customs. Our friend seemed to be looking around for something to use to crack it open, but Gale was ahead of him and reached into his own pocket producing a pocket knife.

"How can you open a coconut with a pocket knife?" I asked, but the Armenian sailor took it and started to pry at the tough shell.

By now I was feeling the effects of the brandy, and I was sure that Gale and the sailor were in the same shape. In addition to our being a little unsteady from the booze, the train was jostling us about on the not-too-smooth railroad tracks, so when the next rough turn came up, the knife slipped, and produced a rather nasty cut in the sailor's hand. He dropped the coconut and the open knife and said something in a foreign language that would have no doubt made an Armenian sailor blush. He took out a not-too-clean handkerchief from his jacket pocket. I offered him some brandy which he drizzled on the wound before he wrapped his hand in the hanky. Gale and I just stared at each other wondering what next.

He picked the coconut back up, and looked around again.

"Ah!" he proclaimed as he walked over to a small metal door in the sidewall of the train car.

He opened up the door to reveal, which to my electrical engineering trained eye, looked like an electrical panel. Gale took a swig of his vodka, dribbling a little from the corner of his mouth onto the floor.

The Armenian sailor ran his finger along the thin edge of the panel door. A satisfied "humph" came out from pursed lips as he nodded his head up and down.

Before I could say *be careful you don't hit the electrical breakers*, he started to tap the coconut shell against the door edge.

After a few test taps, he made a really hard rap against the panel, and the coconut split in two. Before he could turn the two halves sideways to catch the juice, it splattered all over, hitting the panel, the floor, and his clothes.

"Jesus!" I said, jumping back, expecting a big fireball to come from the electrical panel, now dripping in coconut juice.

The Armenian started to laugh with Gale joining in. As I was about to join in their laughter, a large babushka of a woman, came through the door from the adjoining car. The laughter immediately stopped. She was wearing a conductor's uniform and one of those head scarves that all the Russian women seemed to wear, especially the larger of the species, which included almost all of them.

Gale and I gave each other a look meaning "this is it, we did it now" as we inched toward each other in a move of solidarity trying to distance ourselves from the Armenian. The conductor looked down at the mess on the metal floor, which now had coconut juice mixed with the blood and booze all swirling around an open pocket knife. The conductor pointed with one hand to the floor, and the other to the open electrical panel. In Russian, she proceeded to chew out the sailor who had half of a coconut in each hand, one of which was wrapped in a blood-soaked hanky. When she bent down to pick up the knife, he just stepped on it blocking her from doing so.

Well, I guess our man of the world was not about to take any crap from this woman. He proceeded to chew right back in Russian waving dripping coconut halves, backing down the conductor. She said a few more words, none of which was "puzhalsta" or "spasiba" and threw a scowling glance our way. She then stormed out of the room and into the car with the Komsomol girls, whom she could more easily intimidate. The Armenian made some sort of hand gesture toward the parting babushka which I can't describe, but it must have meant something really nasty in his country. He handed me the only coconut with any remaining juice in it and, with a wave of his wounded hand, indicated that I drink from it. He then bent down and retrieved the open knife.

Straightening back up, he proceeded to gouge out a chunk of coconut meat from the other half. I took a drink of the juice and chased it down with some brandy. The Armenian looked on approvingly as I handed my coconut half to Gale who also took a drink and chased it with vodka. Gale traded his coconut half for the meat in the Armenian's hand, took a bite and handed it to me.

"Good, huh?" the Armenian asked.

"Duh, duh," we both responded in unison. Apparently duh means yes in Armenian too, or he didn't want to correct us. I passed my bottle to him with the remaining meat, and he followed our example with the drink-eat-drink-some-more routine. He put what remained of the two coconuts in his bag and my attention returned to his belt.

I pulled out my passport and offered to trade it for his belt. I wasn't worried, about losing my passport, or didn't care because of the brandy. I had three passports; the travel-to-communist-Russia-only-one-time passport which the Russians had taken in Yokohama harbor when we went on board the Russian ship, Felix Dzerzhinsky (technically Russian territory); my official military passport which Sally held; and my regular travel passport. I had offered him my travel passport, knowing I could get another if I reported it stolen.

"Mah-cha mon-yea," he repeated, but then he pointed to my watch.

Apparently, we had just entered the bargaining phase where *mah-cha mon-yea* meant it was worth the price of an American watch. I was not drunk enough to trade the watch my parents had given to me when I had graduated from high school. Inscribed on the back was my graduation date, and it was a nice, self-winding Bulova. I knew it cost my parents $60 in 1962, but it was worth much more to me in sentimental value.

"Nyet," I said, proffering my passport again.

"Mah-cha mon-yea," he said thumbing his belt. I then noticed the gold belt buckle. It could have been real gold, which would have indeed made it worth *mah-cha mon-yea*. I therefore dropped the subject, took another drink of brandy, and handed him the bottle. He finished what little remained as the slowing train approached another station.

"Must go," he said, and held out his arms to give us both hugs and right/left cheek kisses, typical of European hello/goodbyes. He then picked up his bag and headed to the forward car to de-train. Feeling that we were now fully protected from scurvy this day (the bottles were empty), we set the empties down amidst the now drying mess on the floor and headed back to the seats next to our waiting wives.

As we stumbled passed the staring-straight-ahead Komosol girls still sitting bolt upright with their hands folded in their laps, Gale and I looked out the window as the now moving train passed the sailor who was walking toward the station. Our wives had worried looks on their faces, which got worse as I told her about the failed attempt to trade my passport. Gale and I then nodded off for the rest of the trip to Leningrad.

Chubbay Cheeker And Abba

Our first night at our last stop in Mother Russia was at the Hotel Mockba (pronounced Moskva) in Leningrad/St. Petersburg. It was a new hotel built for tourists. We had our own bathroom with real toilet paper and our own shower. It was still light outside when we had arrived at 9:30 pm, and our next event was dinner at 10:00.

Since the summer solstice occurs somewhere from June 20 to 23, depending on the year, and because we had arrived June 23, the sun was just starting to set. Leningrad is at 59 degrees latitude and the Arctic Circle is at 66 degrees, so the sun during the solstice just circles around heaven all day. It actually stays twilight all night long, but unlike in our hotel in Moscow, we had heavy window curtains to darken our room.

After dinner, most of us stayed in the dining hall where a live band was setting up. They were amazingly good, and played a lot of older songs from the Beatles and also knew some ABBA songs which were popular at the time. So we just sat back, ordered some drinks, and were prepared to dance the night away. The only problem was their accent, which was readily apparent when they started playing *The Twist*, made popular by Chubby Checker in 1960. It's hard to describe their pronunciation of the words in the song, but they sounded a little like this:

Come on babyef leet's do zee tweest
Come on babyef leet's do zee tweest
Take me by zee leetle haand and go like deese
Ee-oh tweest babyef, babyef tweest
Oooh-yeah yust like deese
Come on leetle mees and do zee tweest

It didn't matter to us though, we knew we were nearing the end of the three-week tour and wanted to let down our hair. So, we danced.

Sometime later, they played an ABBA song. We all got up and danced to *Money, Money, Money, it's a rich man's world,* in passable English. During this song, I noticed that in front of the band, on the raised platform, was an upturned hat. Not knowing what it was for, I kept an eye on the hat after we sat back down.

While the band played another song, we reminisced on the highlights of our trip with others in the group. Turning toward the stage I noticed that someone from a table other than our groups tossed some money in the hat.

That's what the hat's for, I thought. *It's a beggin' hat for donations to the band.*

My curiosity satisfied, I turned back to my companions. A minute or two after the band finished the song, they started another.

The familiar Money, Money, Money sound came out of the speakers and we all looked at each other as if to say, "What is this? They just played that song previously."

I shrugged it off and went back to the discussions. A minute after they had finished the ABBA song, they started again, and it was the same tune.

"What's going on?" one of the group asked.

Remembering the hat on the platform I said, "They want donations in that hat, so they're basically up there begging."

All eyes turned to the hat which no one was approaching to drop cash into. When the band finished the song, after another pause, they played the same song again.

I said, "Let's dance to it every time it's played."

With that said, the group got up and we danced. The band played ABBA again, and we danced again. This went on for the rest of the night. It was a contest to see who would give out first, the band or a group of travel-hardened young Americans, hell bent on winning the battle of the bands and dancers. For sure, no one gave the band any more money, money, money.

Neither of us gave in. We danced and they played the same ABBA song the rest of the night. When it was closing time, we were tired and the band was frustrated, so it was off to bed.

The rest of the visit to Leningrad, June 24th – 25th, was uneventful with cold rainy days. We saw more church museums, the Hermitage, and the Peter and Paul Fortress. June 26th was sunny and we were fortunate as that was the day we toured the Summer Palace built by Peter the Great. It was fabulous and even had fountains fed by a system of pipes from higher elevations in the mountains and needed no pumps. Two more church museums later and it was time for our farewell-to-Russia dinner. After dinner, we stayed and danced, this time to a different band; no beggin' hat, and no ABBA. We turned in at midnight.

The next morning was our trip to the Russian/Finnish border, leaving at 8:45 and arriving at the border crossing at 1:00. Along the way we were treated to a boxed lunch that the hotel had packed for us. It was a parting shot of cucumbers, eggs, salami, and dark bread. While the border guards were gathering our passports and scrutinizing every face to make sure we matched the person depicted in the passport picture, we discovered that the bus to take us to freedom was two hours away at a town called Vyborg. Our tour guide and escort were able to contact the bus, but we had to wait on the old bus for the entire time. It was forbidden to get out and merely walk across the border to wait on the other side.

Finally, when our other bus had arrived, we were permitted to go through customs. All of our luggage and hand carry was checked thoroughly. It was forbidden to take out more money than you had brought with you and rubles had to remain in Russia. I had my stash of rubles in my socks and made it to freedom with a sample of worthless money.

Like most Japanese travelers, our guide, Paul, wore a money belt and was ordered to drop trou, was frisked, and his money belt was searched. Ecstatically, about 4:30, we left Mother Russia and were going through Finnish customs where nothing was checked.

As soon as we crossed the border the sun came out, the sky cleared, the birds chirped, and the countryside was green and flowery. Every house was different and colorful. There were billboards, signs, supermarkets, department stores, and all the things missing from Communist Russia.

Breaking out the Champagne and wine, we had a wonderfully relaxing three-hour trip to Helsinki while our very pleasant Finnish representative answered any questions we had had.

Lenin's Tomb

Lenin's Tomb was in the middle of Red Square, a solemn monument to the leader of the Glorious October Revolution. According to our guide, it was supposedly revered by all Russians. It could be compared to the Tomb of the Unknowns in Arlington Cemetery as far as importance to the Russian people. So, when I almost burst out laughing not ten feet from the open sarcophagus, I might have been shot on the spot. Let me explain.

Two days after I had dropped my rocks in the limnological museum at Lake Baikal, we were taken to Red Square in Moscow. The tour this day included a trip to Lenin's Tomb where we would view another dead leader of the Glorious October Revolution. The line was long, but because we were with a tour group we were ushered to the front of the line. Sally and I again teamed up with Heidi and Gale.

In front of us was a slow procession of tourists and Russians all queued up to see Lenin resting in state. He had been resting since his death in 1924. Mao Tse-Tung had only been dead a year when we had viewed him in his mausoleum in Tiananmen Square in Peking, which is now Beijing. Mao's exposed, embalmed skin had looked waxen after such a short time, so we thought that Lenin, after 53 years, must really be ripe.

Lenin's tomb and sarcophagus are still in Red Square and open to the public. The descendants of the embalmers state that the corpse is real and requires daily care. The exposed parts are moisturized and preservatives are injected under the clothes. The sarcophagus is kept at 61 degrees and the humidity is controlled between 80 to 90 percent.

Every 18 months, the corpse is given a chemical bath and disinfected. Other chemicals are used to eliminate dark spots on the face and hands, and the color is maintained with hydrogen peroxide. When it was feared that the Germans might damage the corpse, it was moved in October, 1941, to Siberia for safe keeping. After the war it was returned to Red Square.

Stalin was also embalmed and laid next to Lenin, but was removed in the early 60's before our trip.

Even though we were ushered to the front of the outside line, there was a line inside. In fact, we waited another hour and a half in that line before we got to the chamber where Lenin lay in a coffin open from the chest up. Lining the entrance and exit and on all four corners of the coffin were very grim looking Russian soldiers standing guard. They were smartly dressed, complete with rifles. If anyone had tried anything, either that would be the last thing they tried, or they wouldn't see the light of day for the rest of their lives.

It was at this solemn moment that Gale decided to whisper in my ear.

"Try dropping your rocks in here," he said.

I almost lost it. For one thing, his whispers in the dead silent room attracted the attention of a couple of the guards. The image of me dropping my rocks seemed funny and I had to fight back one of those stifled laughs that sounds like someone trying to start a car with a bad solenoid. All I could think of was to take out a handkerchief, cover my nose and mouth, and pretend I was starting to cry for the Bolshevik leader. Sally and Heidi looked at me as though they thought I was crazy, but no one said a word as it is forbidden to talk in the tomb chamber. Gale was pretending that nothing was out of the ordinary.

My theatrics must have done the trick as the guards turned their eyes away from me. When we were safely away from the tomb, I finally let loose. I good humouredly chided Gale for trying to get me killed or thrown into a Siberian prison for the rest of my life. He just shrugged his shoulders.

Moutai

Right after President Nixon opened up China for travel by U.S. citizens in the late seventies, my wife and I visited the communist country. We were with a tour group that traveled from Hong Kong to Beijing via Shanghai and saw a lot of China along the way.

We had taken several trips during our five years when I was working on Okinawa for the federal government. We visited Russia, Thailand, Singapore, Taiwan, and Macao, to name a few. On those tours there was precious little time to wander around by ourselves, as everything was planned for us, including places to eat.

However, we always managed to get away during the free periods, and the China trip was no exception. One evening in Beijing, we walked into what could only be called a bar connected to the hotel where we had been staying. Some older Chinese men walked in as we were sampling some of the locally made beer of unremarkable quality.

They ordered something from the bar and headed in our direction carrying tumblers of a yellowish tinted liquid. One of them spoke some English and he asked if they could sit with us and talk. We were delighted and welcomed them eagerly.

They were curious about where we had gone in their country and were maybe a little jealous, as travel for natives was restricted in the communistic society. I was curious what they were drinking and posed the question.

"Moutai" was the response.

He had pronounced the "mou" part of the word the same as saying their deceased leaders name, Mao, and the second part as "tie." Earlier in the day we had viewed the body of Mao, lying in repose at Tiananmen Square in the center of the city. The image of the waxen looking leader was still fresh in our minds. It was a surprise to us to notice how large a man Chairman Mao had been. It was unusual, too, when compared to the size of the average Chinese male which was around five two with a weight under one hundred-fifty pounds.

Our newly acquired friends noticed our inquisitiveness and were eager for us to have a taste of the beverage found only in their country. When new rounds were ordered, we found to our delight that a glass of Moutai had been purchased for each of us. My wife was not as brave as I was, so I sampled the beverage first. I took a whiff, as if it were a fine wine to be first experienced by the nose. I could only describe the odor as like that of kerosene, but refrained from any reaction that would offend our hosts.

"Hmm," I said, exhaling vigorously through my nostrils in an effort to get the vapors outside of my body before someone lit a match and I spewed forth flame like a dragon. The two men were eagerly watching me, encouraging me with their eyes to take a sip. So I did, while avoiding any effort to breathe in.

It was god-awful! There was no describing the flavor as I fought off the effort of my throat to cleanse itself. Through extreme effort, I was able to swallow without convulsing. There was an immediate burning sensation from the tip of my tongue to the pit of my stomach.

"Very nice," I said, as soon as my vocal chords came out of an epileptic seizure.

"It is very nice, the Moutai," the one who brought the drinks said, bobbing his head in a gesture of agreement instead of questioning.

"Wonderful," I lied.

Our attention was drawn to my companion as it was her turn. We had been together for eight years and like most married couples she could tell when I was not being truthful. I have to give her "A" for bravery as she took a sip herself. She was at least smart enough not to sniff it first, after noticing that my eyes had welled up with tears. Like me, she had been able to get it down her throat and thus avoided a major diplomatic faux pas, but now, we were trapped.

So as not to embarrass ourselves and label our country as a nation of wimps so soon after Americans had been given permission to visit inside China, we had to finish our drinks. While carrying on additional conversation, we were able to sip our way to empty glasses, thus avoiding an international incident. I have to admit though, that once my throat became numb, it went down a lot easier. We graciously turned down another Moutai each with the excuse that we had to get up early in the morning to visit the Great Wall, a partial truth, as we were going to go to the Wall the next day, but did not have to get up early.

With the smell of kerosene on our breath, we hurried to our rooms and brushed our teeth until our gums were sore. Surprisingly, we had not suffered adversely from the effects of Moutai and there had been no woozy feeling or hangover.

In mid-morning, we got on a bus to head for the Great Wall of China. Nothing more needs to be said about our destination as it is one of the Seven Wonders of the World. The section opened up to tourists had been renovated as the four thousand mile long wall was in disrepair. The wall is located in a remote section of China where repairs, should they be attempted along the entire wall, would be cost prohibitive. Therefore, the Peoples Republic only repaired the portion that was open to the public.

We arrived in a valley and the sight of the wall was incredible, seeming to loom larger as we got closer. It is fifteen to thirty feet high and about fifteen feet wide. We climbed the stairway on the China side (there was no stairway, for good reason, on the Mongolian side). The wall rose in both the east and west direction almost straight up the sides of the mountainous terrain. The wall was constructed so that three mounted horses could ride side by side from one end to the other. It was hard to believe that a horse could run along such a steep incline. It was difficult for us just to walk up. In unison, Sally and I decided to climb as high up as we could on the east side, which appeared to be the only side opened to the public. We started our trek.

For the occasion, I had worn a special T-shirt. It was a Kliban cat shirt as shown below.

Two cats clad in Mao jackets and hats on a yellow background were pictured in front of a mouse hole. On the floor in front of the mouse hole, was some "specs." The cat away from the mouse hole was saying "Mao," an imitation of meow. The cat bending down and looking at the specs on the floor was saying "Mousie dung," as in Mao Tse Tung, an obvious slur on the deceased Chinese leader's name. Had they understood what was on the shirt, I could have been shot or hauled off to some prison where I would still be making Mattel toys as part of my rehabilitation.

As we climbed to the lofty perch to where the picture was taken, we passed by some awful sights in the nooks and crannies of the Wall. As stated before, the Chinese spit a lot. In addition to dribbles of saliva, we also passed by where someone had defecated. That would be the equivalent of pooping in a corner of the stairwell on the Washington monument.

Having completed our climb and the steep descent back to our starting point, we returned to the bus just as it was time to leave. On the way back, since there were no restaurants near the wall, we were given a box lunch prepared for us by the hotel. Now there is probably a revolving restaurant near the place we stopped to take the picture of me in my T-shirt.

After we returned from the Great Wall, I was able to find a bottle of Moutai in the hotel gift store and I bought a 106 proof, 9.2 ounce bottle. The bottle is ceramic, which I surmised is necessary since glass would be etched away and metal would be dissolved by the caustic contents. I still have the unopened bottle which has written on the back in Chinese and perfectly good English the following:

"Moutai is one of China's renowned liquors which enjoys acclaim both at home and abroad. Production of Moutai began in 1704 in the town of that name in the Renhuai County, Kweichow province. Selected wheat, the choicest sorghum and the excellent local water goes into its preparation. Traditional brewing expertise, together with long aging, gives Moutai its characteristically distinct bouquet."

Bouquet? We obviously had drunk an inferior batch of Chinese white lightning made from fermented dragon droppings.

Chinese Toilets and the Art of Looking The Other Way

My first encounter with the oriental lack of discretion with bathroom protocol was in the airport at the Tokyo International Airport, not the one at Narita, but the old one at Haneda. I entered the only restroom that I could find, and saw upright urinals, so it must be the men's room. As I was almost done relieving myself, I heard another patron come in and I half turned my head to see who it was. I almost stopped in mid stream as I noticed that it was a woman.

I must be in a men's room, I thought. *I'm standing at a urinal.*

My previous experience with Japanese bathrooms was one of awe at the in-the-floor urinals that were used for everything. There were no seats, and one had to squat to do what comes naturally. But this was a shocker. When I left, I noticed that it was a unisex restroom where the men either used the stalls or the urinals, and the women just walked by the men at the urinals to use the stalls.

This still did not prepare me for the bathrooms in China.

"I have to go potty," I told my wife.

We had just finished our tour of the Tiger Balm gardens, a gruesome display of Chinese Gargoyles munching on people. What that has to do with the mentholated type of balm with the same name, I don't know, but the gardens were on the list of things to do in Hong Kong, so we went.

We always tried to relieve ourselves in the comfort of the hotel and refrained from drinking anything until we got to a nice restaurant or back to the hotel. We knew that toilets in the Far East are not for the weak of stomach. So far I had avoided having to use the local facilities, but I knew I couldn't wait any longer.

Shortly after arriving in Japan, we had learned how to ask for the facilities in Japanese. The only word we had learned for toilet was benjo, and doka desku was "where is." So we put the two together as in benjo, doka desku, only we didn't know that the direct translation is something like "where's the shithouse?" Benjo can also refer to the concrete-covered and sometimes open ditches that run along the streets where everything from sewage to rainwater enters. We did not know how to ask for a toilet in Chinese.

"I think that's one?" Sally said, pointing to a small building in the alleyway with a doorless entryway.

I watched as men went in with gotta-go looks on their faces and came out with relieved looks.

"I'll try it," I said, a little apprehensively.

After all, I convinced myself, I had used the pub bathrooms in Scotland where I and the other sailors just pissed against a wall where occasionally water cascaded from a tank near the ceiling to wash away the waste. Approaching the shack cautiously, I prepared myself for what I would or wouldn't find inside. No amount of imagination could have conjured up what I saw when I finally entered.

The first thing I noticed was that there were no lights. Illumination came from the outside through slits in the walls. There were partitions, thank God for that, but there were no urinals (I didn't expect any), nor were there any toilets, not even the kind in Japan that looked like urinals installed horizontally on the floor. What I saw was a trough of running water in the middle of each stall going from the stall at the far end of the unlighted shack to a hole near the entrance. Just then I heard grunting at the end stall

Oh my God, I thought. *Do I really have to do this*, to which my bladder answered, "Either that or wet your pants."

I entered the first stall and slid my pants down. I didn't want to stand up and piss as the stalls were only about four feet high. If someone had come in and noticed me, I might not have been able to finish from embarrassment. Americans are accustomed to privacy and sitting on something to do their business. Orientals are used to just squatting, sometimes in public. Even when I was a kid, going to the bathroom outside, we sat over a log or against a tree for support. Now I had to squat and try to keep from falling into the abyss below me.

I got one knee bent more than the other and rested my forearms on my thighs. Just as I started to go, I heard another grunt from the man further upstream and a plopping sound.

"Upstream!" I said, in a gasp.

Just as the realization hit me, I looked down and saw the cause of the plopping sound come floating by on top of the running water. Somehow I was able to control my disgust and finish what I had reluctantly come into the shack for in the first place. In my haste to leave, almost knocking an entering patron down in the process, I did not notice if there had been any toilet paper in the stalls.

"Oh my God!" Sally said, as I told her what it was like. "You'd better be upstream the next time."

"There ain't gonna be a next time," I said. "I'll go into a dark alleyway first and take my chances on getting mugged."

On our trip across China, we found out the mainland Chinese are even more unabashed in their elimination habits. One day for lunch we were all escorted to an authentic Chinese restaurant. Of course it was authentic, it was in China. Sitting twelve at a round table, we were presented with our meal which consisted of large platters loaded with unidentifiable concoctions. It was family style and we passed the platters around taking what we wanted from each.

Sally and I were facing the open entrance across from which was another open room. I at first thought that the adjacent room was another dining room. People went into the room and seemed to sit down behind partitions above which I could see their heads, but they didn't stay long. Then the realization came to me.

"Do you know what that room is over there," I said to Sally, gesturing with a nod of my head.

"No what?" she asked.

"Benjo, doka desku," I said.

"No!" she said, just as another user of the facility stood up and adjusted his pants.

Then the disgusted snickers started as the others who had overheard us came to the same realization. Those people were doing their business with their heads in plain view of those of us eating lunch.

One other disgusting habit about the Chinese men is that they are constant spitters. Not only do they spit constantly, but they hack up luggies just before they let fly. Walking down the street in Shanghai, we noticed that in front of every public building was a spittoon. Being Americans, we were not used to seeing spittoons except in the old cowboy movies. Therefore, we couldn't help but to look at them when we walked by. What was in there was disgusting and not worth describing, nor could I. What I witnessed that day was another example of Chinese habits. I saw a mother hold her child over a spittoon to do what children do. I also saw one being held over an open storm sewer for the same purpose.

It took some time, but we soon learned the lesson of quickly looking away when we saw something unbelievable to the western civilization-trained eye.

I realize that there are a lot of Chinese, but I do hope, since our trip in 1989, that with their new found status in the world, they have adopted some of the American bathroom manners from the people who buy a lot of their products.

PART FOUR

Pot Porridge

The Three Wise Camels

(A Christmas Story for the 21ˢᵗ Century)

"Harrumph!" exclaimed Fred the camel, grumbling as camels often do. "Where are we headed now?"

"I don't know," Jack, the second camel, grumbled back. "Let's ask Frank, he knows everything."

Frank the third and largest of the three camels was in front of the other two. Frank was always in front. His rider, Gaspar, was the leader of the trio that on most nights always headed to the local oasis and its open-air Kasbah, The Camel and Rider, to watch television on the big-screen plasma TV. The camels didn't much care for the popular show, CSI, Camels Saving Islam, or the other shows on most other nights, but they did like to watch the local polo game played on camels and sponsored by Ships of the Desert aftershave which was on every Monday night.

"How about it, Frank," Jack asked. "Where are these camel jockeys taking us now?"

"You know they don't like to be called that," Frank answered in his booming deep voice. "But to answer you, I overheard Melchior tell Balthazar that we were following a star."

"A star!" Fred exclaimed in disbelief. For his size, Fred was a little heavier than the other two and a little lazier, as camels go. "Why are we crossing the desert following a star?"

"It has something to do with a Messiah who is supposed to be a very special king of some sort," Frank replied. "His birth was predicted to happen soon and they think it's tomorrow morning."

"I see the star," Jack said, looking up into the desert sky. "That sure looks like a long way from here. I haven't had a drop of water in three days, and my hump is running on empty." Jack was small and skinny, as far as camels go, and his hump did not hold as much reserve water as the other two.

"The star is only to show us which direction to go," Frank said, turning his head to the left to address Jack. "If it's any comfort to you, Jack, I can smell water coming from an oasis, so we are not too far from the place now." Before he could turn back around, Gaspar gave him a kick in his ribs to shut him up. The riders couldn't understand camel talk, but they could hear them grunting and grumbling. Camels were expected to hush up and march, and tonight the riders had to get to their destination.

"My load is heavy gold," Fred said, in a whisper. Although his ribs could absorb the shock a lot better, he did not want to get a kick such as Frank had just received. "You don't hear me complaining. You two are carrying that smelly stuff, which is a lot lighter."

"Lighter, but just as valuable as the gold you carry," Frank said.

"What is this smelly stuff?" Jack asked.

"It's frankincense and myrrh," Frank said. "They are both tree sap that comes from Somalia, a country on the east coast of Africa. They are very expensive and worth their weight in gold. These are gifts fit for a king."

"I don't care," Fred said. "Your loads are still lighter than mine. What is that sappy stuff used for?"

"It is burned as incense for rituals and worship," Frank answered. "It gives off a pleasant odor, not like what comes from you, Fred."

"Oh great!" Fred exclaimed, ignoring the nasty remark. "They'll burn your load and I'll still have to carry this heavy gold around."

Frank responded. "They are gifts and we are to leave them when we get there. Stop your bellyaching. See, we're almost there." Frank raised his left front hoof to point, which earned him another kick.

"It is not my belly, it is my hump which is aching with thirst," Fred complained, a little too loudly. This also earned him a kick which added to the pain of carrying the gold. The three decided to be quiet until they got to their destination. No camel liked to be kicked in the ribs.

In the desert, distances could fool you. The destination, an oasis, with a stable beside it, in the little town of Bethlehem, about five miles south of Jerusalem, had looked close when the camels last spoke, but it took two hours to get there. They arrived well after midnight. As they approached, a beam of light from the star shot down from the sky through a skylight in the stable, illuminating a manger.

"Look at that," Frank said very softly, which sounded to the riders like a deep sigh.

"Oh my God!" Fred said forgetting his heavy load and his thirsty hump.

"Yes, precisely," Frank responded. The riders were in such awe and reverence they allowed the camels to voice their opinions without any more kicking.

As the riders dismounted and took their gifts of gold, frankincense, and myrrh with them to present to the man and woman kneeling next to the manger, the camels heard, "Welcome to the birth of Christ the Savior," which seemed to come from the manger.

"A talking manger," Jack said. "You don't see many of those anymore."

"Shush!" came a chorus of voices. The other animals could also talk; and the sheep, cattle, and goats all turned to see the newcomers. Standing to one side with their staffs in their hands were other men, who looked like shepherds and must have brought the sheep,

"Please allow us to ask just what has happened," Frank said, as politely as possible.

The manger responded. "This humble baby was born this morning to Mary and her husband Joseph, but he is also born to all of us. There was no place for them at the inn because of all the visitors, so Mary and Joseph came to this stable, bore him, wrapped him in this cloth, and placed him in me. I am so honored. In time he will do many miraculous things and eventually will save us from our sins. He is the Son of God and is named Jesus of Nazareth."

Just as the manger had finished telling his short story, the baby, with the light beaming down onto his face from the brightest star all had ever seen, turned his head toward the camels and all the other visitors and raised his right hand as if to say "Welcome."

There was a great silence all around. More than they had ever experienced before, the camels, all the other animals, and the men felt a great love and warmth.

The Beginning

A Bike Vermont Adventure
Introduction

Our fourth bike-riding trip with Bike Vermont in as many years started off like the rest. We checked in to the B&B, the Manchester Highlands Inn, and took our luggage to our room. It was on the third floor so lugging a week's worth of bike-riding gear and miscellaneous clothing gave me, at least, the excuse to have a cookie or two from the B&B's ample cookie jar. We had already done our wine shopping for the trip so there was nothing to do but await the Bike Vermont sag wagon to see if we would have the same tandem as we had had the last three years. But, more importantly, to see who our tour leaders would be.

We didn't have to wait long as the van rolled into the parking lot. There was a lot of blond hair in the driver's seat so I knew one of our tour leaders was not any of the ones we had on previous trips. Oh well, another one to break in and train. Thank the gods the one with the hair was the female. The male emerged from the passenger side and we noticed that we would be training two of them this trip.

We rushed out to greet them and let them get over the shock of meeting us for the first time. The tandem was indeed the same one as before and I still don't know or care what brand it was or what components were installed on it. All I cared about was that I would not have to re-adjust the wheel size of the bike computer I had used last time and brought with us again. The same comfortable saddle was on blue tandem which is important when riding on the rough roads of rural Vermont.

For non-bikers, a tandem is a two-person bike. The person in front is called the captain (who does all the work) and the person in back is called the stoker (who just sits there eating ice cream and reading a book). A tandem can make or break a marriage, so before rushing out to buy one, I recommend renting one first. Also, a computer is an electronic calculator connected to the wheels to let the rider know speed, average speed, maximum speed, time, ride distance, and total distance. They can get quite sophisticated with indications of pedal cadence, heart rate, mach speed, star locations, GPS directions, and directions to Grandma's house.

Our tour leaders turned out to be Saunie and Patrick. After being introduced, I immediately intoned Saunie, Saunie, Saunie as in that ancient sitcom, Bosom Buddies, where Tom Hanks said Sunny, Sunny, Sunny too many times to forget. Saunie had no idea what I was alluding to since she was from a younger (maybe two) generation(s). Our training of the tour guides had begun. Patrick, a former anchorman for Fox, on the other hand looked younger than he actually was and had many stories to tell, including the one where he interviewed Muhammad Ali, not once, but twice in the same day. At least Bike Vermont provided us with a variety of interesting tour guides.

We also found out there were only two other couples on tour with us. And guess what? One of the couples (Alex and Allison) was from the Dallas area. We were also from the Dallas area. The other two, John and Charlotte, were from Baltimore and had been on a Bike Vermont tour before. This was a first for us since all the other tours had had five or six other couples. Oh well, I have a bad enough time remembering names anyway. At least I could remember Saunie, Saunie, Saunie and John, which is also my name. As it turned out later, the smaller group size had its advantages.

Before continuing, I want to relate a humorous story about Vermont. It may be humorous, but it gives an idea of the life style, people, and mood of Vermont. On Saturday, the day before the tour started, we arrived in Vermont and immediately noticed signs at almost every general store urging "Vote for Fred." Some signs added "The Man with a Plan." We thought this was a joke of some sort but found out later that 79-year-old Fred Tuttle, was running for the Republican Senatorial nomination. We were also told that he had had a movie made about him, *The Man with a Plan.*

He did win his race while we were there. With limited access to TV and radio (the best way to vacation) we got sketchy details about what had happened. We found out that Fred was unhappy because a millionaire, who had only been in the state for less than three years, was running for a U.S. Senate seat. Fred vowed to run against him to prevent "outsiders" from ruining the state. He promised to only spend $16 in his election effort. He later apologized for over spending by about $180, but said most of that was for the portable toilets he had to rent for the fifty-cents-a-plate dinner at his house. Most people didn't care that he did not keep his limited-spending promise, since his opponent had spent over $400,000.

When interviewed on TV after winning the election, he was asked what he was going to do next. He stated that he guessed he would now have to run for Senator against the incumbent Democrat. Fred, forgive me if I did not get the story entirely correct, but this was one of the many stories we had heard that made us want to live out the rest of our lives in Vermont. Now back to the biking adventure.

Weather is always a concern on these trips and on a five-day tour we were bound to have some rain, especially in the fall. It didn't matter since we had brought our rain gear, towels, and an extra pair of shoes. We had had rain on our first Vermont biking trip four years earlier and had learned quickly what clothing to bring for unexpected weather.

I took advantage of the time before dinner to install the computer on the back of the tandem. The computer gives the stoker something to do to occupy her time and that's good. It also lets her know how fast we are going and that's bad, which I will demonstrate later. I'd like to say that we had the most expensive computer on the market, but I can't because it was on sale from Nashbar for under $20. And hey, the batteries still worked after four years. Enough of this techno talk. Let's get to the heart of the trip, the food.

The food is the best part of a biking trip. As Patrick said, I bike so that I can eat more. I could tell right then that he had a way with words. It turns out he was going to produce a TV series on biking across America, or bike tours in general, or something like that. Anyway, back to the basics. I don't remember what we had the first night, but our hostess had once taught a thing or three to Julia Child and she had the photos to prove it. Every meal we had at the B&B had some sort of edible flowers on the plate. So I had my fill of bushes and twigs (that's what I called anything served that wasn't meat, fat, starch, or sugar). The flowers had no taste, except for the onion flower (if hot can be called taste), but they sure were "purdy to eat."

Day One

The first day for riding was on Monday, September 7 which also happened to be Labor Day. Manchester, Vermont, the outlet capital of the northeast, was a busy little town. We only crossed the main highway coming into town once on our way out. We passed by Al Ducci's, which is an Italian food store that has more kinds of Italian edible things than most stores in a big town. After our move to Vermont you can bet that we planned to visit Al Ducci's and Ba Ba Louie's bakery near Chester Vermont. Remember, bike to eat.

Riding past the Amtrak station gave us the opportunity to give a toot on our Rails-to-Trails train whistle. The whistle really sounds authentic and when used in the country it scares the dickens out of chickens, cows, goats, pigs, and tour leaders, especially when they are crossing railroad tracks. No, I am not the type who puts a lampshade on his head at parties.

It was a relief leaving town on the downhill side, knowing we would not return that way, but the law of physics always comes into play. You know, what goes down, must come up, especially when we would be returning to the same B&B that night. Our route meandered through the hills and valleys of southern Vermont with Equinox Mountain towering above us. Monday was supposed to be an easy day of 25 miles. There was an option to make it 47 miles, but having ridden in Vermont before, we decided to go the shorter distance and save ourselves for the next day. Or so we thought.

The routes chosen were excellent as usual. We biked on a lightly traveled road half way up the mountains on either side of the valley below. This provided a very scenic way to see the mountains, valleys, and rural farmhouses of Vermont. We also got a taste of the smells of Vermont. I mean this, because we could actually taste the smells, especially when passing the many milk farms along the way. To our amazement, we saw some of the maple trees starting to turn red. Not the blazing red of the peak season, but nonetheless, a peek at the autumn to come in New England.

To give some idea of how "hilly" bike rides in Vermont can be, we were able to average fourteen to sixteen miles per hour on our tandem south of Dallas. This is the hilliest part of the Dallas area, so we are used to some hills. However, in Vermont we only averaged eight to nine miles per hour and this was on the moderate to easy routes. On previous trips, we had not done any of the more difficult rides. Besides, Bike Vermont wouldn't rent us a tandem for the difficult routes and we were not about to bring our own bike. But hey, we went to Vermont for vacation and wanted to have fun, not work hard.

We arrived at the lunch spot about 10:30 in the town of Dorset and parked our tandem at the village green. Immediately the town dog came over to sniff us out and check on our food situation. She didn't like the only food we had, bananas, so she stayed until her curiosity gave out and meandered back to her place in front of the general store.

This is what is so appealing about Vermont. There are friendly people, dogs, and general stores in every little town along the way. The general stores have everything one can think of from bolts to bag balm (a concoction of salve and ointment used on cow's udders to soothe and heal rashes). Where they get the rashes from is a secret kept between the farmer and the cow, but the stuff is also good on bike seat saddle-sores (so I am told).

At about eleven o'clock, Saunie and Patrick arrived at the green in Dorset driving the sag wagon (called that because it "sags" behind the riders carrying tools, clothing, food, and water). We filled our water bottles and for lunch ate the Fig Newtons they had brought, and another banana for the potassium. This was the point where the optional mileage kicked in and since we were halfway through the short ride and didn't feel like eating lunch (saving ourselves for the free dinner and edible bushes and twigs) we inquired about the optional mileage. Saunie, Saunie, Saunie told us that the optional ride included one small hill but the rest was fairly easy. So, off we went about the same time as the other riders were pulling in. I'm not saying they were slower than we were, but they did stop at more places along the way, so we were usually a hop ahead.

Eating a large lunch on a long bike ride is not a good idea. After our first year's bike adventure in Vermont, I learned to eat fruit or a light sandwich when there was still a long way to go. Calories for the long rides are best obtained from sport drinks and/or candy bars. On the first day of that first year's ride I thought I had burned enough calories before lunch to deserve a greasy hamburger and cheese fries. That was a big mistake. About an hour later, I felt like we were towing a cement truck and we still had more than an hour to go. Never again! Ride to eat, but lunch lightly. Unlike a heavy lunch, breakfast never affected me that way because we always had a trip planning meeting with the tour guides before heading out. That hour or two delay allowed the food to digest a little instead of sitting in my stomach like a rock.

Well, off we went on the longer, optional ride. Riding was a breeze heading north and even with a slight headwind, we were cruising at over twenty miles per hour. Remember that I said we averaged less than nine and this day would be no exception. The small hill that we were going up turned into at least an eight-percent grade for more than four miles. Understand that Vermont ain't flat and the roads ain't straight so we could only hope that the top of the hill was around the next bend, and the next, and the next until we had finally reached the top, went over the crest, and started down the other side. Sometimes we even got fooled into thinking we had reached the top (like we did on this route) only to find that it was just a dip before the hill started back up again around the next bend in the road.

We were cranking in granny (forgive me if I get some of the jargon wrong) which is the lowest gear, 1-1 on a mountain tandem with twenty-four gear choices. I wish we had had more, because we had to stop three times to let my heart rate get back down to it's maximum of 165 beats per minute (that's what the charts had said the maximum was for my age). Anyway, we saw a sign for trucks on wedges (think about it) and thought we were on our way down. Think again. At the bottom of this very steep, but short, hill there was another one going up. This was the last downhill we saw for the next two miles. It even got so bad we were trying to judge from the noise of trucks ahead of us how far up we still had to go. We couldn't see more than 100 feet ahead before the road turned or was obstructed by trees.

Well, cranking along at about four miles per, we were running out of water. Hey, we were going to Vermont and didn't need our hydrator backpacks. "'Cause it ain't as hot as Texas in the summer" one of us had said before we had left home in Dallas. Besides, the sag wagon was supposed to be along any minute, or was it. Also, by this time there were clouds everywhere and we started to feel the first drops of rain. We didn't mind riding in the rain since it wasn't our bike, we had brought our rain gear, and where was that damn sag wagon?

We finally crested the "hill" and started down the other side stopping about a third of the way at a general store in Danby Four Corners. We bought sports drinks, candy bars, and made a pit stop. By this time it was threatening rain pretty good so we hopped on our tandem for the rest of the trek. The downhill side was a beautiful winding road and was as steep down as we had gone up. The problem was it was starting to rain a lot and, lo and behold, there was the sag wagon coming in the opposite direction. I gave Saunie, Saunie, Saunie the thumbs down sign. We were out of liquids again, but more than that I wanted to know how much farther we had to go before getting back to the B&B. Riding in the van was not for us, since we were already wet, were not that tired, and wanted to finish this ride so we could eat a big dinner.

I stopped the tandem at the side of the road. The sag wagon pulled alongside and Saunie, Saunie, Saunie told us this was too dangerous a place to stop. So we continued down the hill at thirty plus mph in the driving rain and stopped at the general store in Danby ahead of the van. We tanked up on water and Fig Newtons. Saunie, Saunie, Saunie told us we only had ten, maybe less, miles to ride and that it was all flat. She was right about the flat part, but the ten turned out to be closer to sixteen. In the driving rain with our shoes going squish, squish, squish and carrying about a hundred extra pounds of water-logged clothing, we were anxious to get back for happy hour. It was also getting dangerous as we were on heavily traveled Route 7 and 7a. Thank someone for wide shoulders and the lack of broken glass which was unlike every highway we had ridden our tandem on in Texas.

We did finally make it back to the B&B about the same time that it quit raining. Our tour leaders told us that we were the only ones who had done the extra miles (no surprise). Patrick said we were awesome (did I mention he was from California) for doing the extra miles. I just felt wet and wanted to rib Saunie, Saunie, Saunie for lying to us about the "hill" and the distance. But first, I wanted to get a shower and don some dry clothes, then get a beer, some wine, and some brownies, and cookies (not necessarily in that order).

Dinner was wonderful with bushes and twigs and lots of calories. Surprisingly we all retired rather early. I had dreams of sugarplums in my ears and the upcoming breakfast. We got up in time for breakfast of more bushes and twigs. The day's weather looked like there was no chance of rain and our tour guides were providing us with lunch. Oh boy, more food!

Day Two

Tuesday's planned route was longer than Monday's and there were no options. We cycled north out of Manchester and rode on some of the same roads that we had ridden the day before on the optional route. When we got to the turn for the eight-percent grade which we had taken yesterday on the ride from hell, we went straight. Today's route took us further north along an easier road to Danby Four Corners. First, we stopped for lunch at a small town called Middletown Springs. Saunie, Saunie, Saunie provided lunch. I guess Patrick was designated "sweep" on his own bike for the entire week which meant that he had to stay with or behind the last of the riders. Anyway, she had provided an eclectic lunch.

That's right, more bushes and twigs. I remembered the lunch because the other John got sick that evening and we were trying to figure out just what Saunie, Saunie, Saunie had fed us that had made him sick. We decided it was the something-stuffed multi-colored tortellini because it couldn't have been the homemade mozzarella and grass sandwich on whole pumpernickel, wheat-grain, corn-imbedded bread with some kind of unidentifiable sauce that had made him sick. She also had tortilla chips and salsa as a staple for the rest of us. The salsa was made in New York City (a real sneer maker for Texans).

Anyway, right after lunch we took off again toward Danby Four Corners. Saunie, Saunie, Saunie told us that the uphill going out of Middletown Springs was a steep one and Allison decided to ride the sag wagon to the top. Sally and I cringed at the thought of riding to the top of what Saunie, Saunie, Saunie called a steep hill considering she called yesterday's hill small. Turns out she was wrong again. The hill was a wimpy thing by Vermont standards, but I had had another problem before we got to Danby Four Corners. The lunch was a little heavier than I had expected and the old cement truck grabbed on to our bike again. At one point I had to get off to see if the brakes were dragging. Sally swears she was pedaling, so it must have been the lunch. Never again will I eat a lot for lunch while riding (I've said that before).

We finally got to the Danby Four Corners with Patrick close behind riding sweep. We knew the rest was downhill (having ridden it the day before) and, knowing my penchant for speed on the downhill, Sally chose to make a pit stop. I think she was afraid of not being able to hold her bladder if we hit speeds approaching sixty mph. Taking off from the Four Corners general store, my stoker forgot to put up the kickstand and to stop us, I jammed on the brakes really hard causing her to pitch forward almost falling off the bike. Needless to say, there was a lot of wailing and gnashing of teeth. I looked behind and Patrick was hiding behind the general store trying to let us work out our differences ourselves. That tactic must be on the first page of the manual for tour guides. It had been our only tandem-riding argument of the year, if you can believe that.

With, the kickstand up and the old lady in the saddle, we were off again. About a quarter of a mile into the downhill, there was a detour sign saying the bridge further down the road was out. We had been warned about this at our breakfast get together, but we had just been on that road the day before and there was no detour. We had discussed this with Patrick and made a command decision to head on past the detour and take our chances with the bridge. We were also way behind the pack and didn't want to come in too far behind the rest, so off we went hitting thirty plus mph and leaving Patrick in our wake. When we got to the bridge, it was open for us to pass so we zipped on by before someone could say we couldn't. Rejoining the road on the other side of the bridge was Alex and Allison and we flew by them, tooting our train whistles. They took the detour, which must have added a few miles, so that now we wouldn't be the last ones in after all. No one can catch a tandem on the downhill, even with a screaming stoker yelling "slow down" at the top of her lungs. Did I mention I don't hear so well?

At the bottom of the hill was the town of Danby and our second B&B, the Silas Griffith Inn. Mileage this day had been forty-four. The inn was a nice comfortable B&B with a bar and big dining area in converted stables. The woodwork throughout was really nice and the main house had a huge round wooden door, which slid into the wall.

Silas Griffith, Vermont's first millionaire, had been the original owner and had run the logging industry in the area. He had also owned the entire mountainside, Mount Tabor, opposite the B&B. We were amazed by the trucks roaring by, carrying massive blocks of Vermont marble from the near-by quarry.

After cleaning up, we went for a walk and noticed a vegetable garden in back of the inn. We went over to admire it. An elderly man came out to talk to us and explained how bad the weather had been such that his garden was in bad shape. However, we thought it was in great shape. We talked to him for awhile and had mentioned that we came from Texas where we can't have a garden because it's so hot.

"Texas is a terrible place," was his response.

See, word gets around. He had to leave us when his wife came out and told him his dinner was ready.

Dinner for us was lots and lots with wine and dessert. We ordered from a menu that actually had some pretty good choices. This is when the other John got sick just before he got to eat any dinner. We all started to worry about whether it was lunch or some virus that we all would get. John wasn't the only one with a stomach problem. Because I had an upset stomach, either from lunch or riding before the lunch digested, I had taken an antacid.

The only other one who had gotten sick the rest of the trip was John's wife, Charlotte. This ruled out any contagious virus. Patrick may have guessed the possible culprit. His theory was that they had ridden across the road where some of the barnyard stuff had washed out the day before from the heavy rains. When John and Charlotte, had ridden over the stuff, the wheels splashed it onto their bottles and they had ingested it when they drank (they really got a taste of Vermont). Lucky for them, Alex was a doctor so he wrote a prescription to make them feel better.

Day Three

The next day we were supposed to ride up the hill we had come down the day before. The option was for the van to take us all the way to the top so we could ride down the other side, into the state of New York, and then on to our next B&B back in Vermont. We all decided to go with the option since this was not a training week and we had had enough hills. However, Mother Nature had different plans in the form of rain. It started raining before we headed out. John opted to stay at the B&B to recover from, let's just say, a bad night.

By the time we got to the top of the hill it was raining, not hard, but persistently. Sally and I were the first ones out of the van and we looked at each other, the soaked tandem seats, the gloomy weather, and quickly decided this would not be what we considered five hours of fun. The others agreed and, guess what, it was Saunie, Saunie, Saunie's turn to ride sweep. Is this woman lucky or what? The problem was she had scrimped on food the last two days knowing she was not riding, but this morning she chowed down. She really should not have been concerned about gaining weight since she had told us that she would be riding in Stowe, Vermont with Greg LeMond next week.

Patrick drove us to the next town on the riding route, Pawlet. We all bailed out for hot chocolate at the town coffee shop. We wiped the store out of hot chocolate by the time we had decided to scrub the days ride. It was still raining with no sign of letting up. This was one of the advantages of a small group, since we could all be taxied in the sag wagon at once. Piling back into the van, we drove back to the Silas Griffith Inn, changed clothes, and headed back to get our cars in Manchester. Sally and I decided to visit the Norman Rockwell Museum in Arlington while Alex and Allison went shopping. John and Charlotte stayed at the B&B to let John recuperate.

After our visit to the museum, we headed to the West Mountain Inn in Arlington. This turned out to be the best B&B so far. They had a full cookie jar, but also had the best coffee. Green Mountain Coffee Roasters in Waterbury, Vermont was their distributor. I'm not kidding when I say the best. I drink only decaf, and they had a hazelnut decaf that was terrific. The inn is huge and we had a great room except that the others had a fireplace. It did get cold enough in the morning to use it, so Sally and I just had to shiver (the hot-water heating system was not on yet). Supposedly, Michael J. Fox had gotten married there so we spent considerable time before dinner going through the photo albums in the lounge area to see if his pictures were included. But wait, there's more.

At dinner we had a menu that I would give four stars, which was appetizers, sorbet (to cleanse the palate), salads, main course, and dessert. What a country! We naturally pigged out, feeling a little guilty about not riding that day, but justified the food orgy by knowing that we would be riding the next day (if it didn't rain). Before dinner, we did get some exercise. We walked to the llama pens and back and looked at the goldfish and frogs in the pond. The llamas were pretty neat and I was able to coax one over to the fence with the promise of something to eat. The only thing I had was sugarless chewing gum, so I offered and he/she partook. I don't know what sex it was as I couldn't pick it up like a gerbil and look under its tail to see if it was a male or female. It seemed to like the gum, so I gave it another stick.

OK, giving a llama chewing gum is not the smartest thing to do. Who knows, they may be allergic to sorbitol, carnauba wax, aspartame, or sodium saccharin. Come to think of it, what are we doing eating this stuff? At least I didn't try to choke a horse like Allison did. The second day she and Alex had stopped by the side of the road to commune with nature. There were places like this all along Vermont's back roads where bike riders stopped and observed farm animals close up and personal. We had done this ourselves on every bike trip we had taken the last three years.

I think Allison was not a country girl for when she picked a handful of weeds and grass and fed the horse, the horse started choking and she feared it would die. I was not there to see what happened, but I think it's kind of hard to choke a horse with grass and weeds. Fearing the horse would choke to death right there in front of her, she grabbed what was still hanging form the horse's mouth and pulled it back out. Thankfully she told us that she was going to be a dermatologist and not a veterinarian.

Day Four

The next day I was up early and went down to the kitchen area by myself and made some hazelnut decaf. After a few minutes the staff brought out some warm-ups to breakfast which I had to taste. They were the best ever. They were pecan maple bars which went down well with the decaf. By this time Alex and Allison had come down and Allison also fell in love with the bars. We stuffed our pockets full for snacks. But wait, it gets better.

Breakfast was as many courses as dinner. There were sticky buns and muffins, a choice of omelets, eggs, ooey-gooey eggs, pancakes, french toast, meats, and yes, dessert. I have never been to a place that served dessert after breakfast. I know Denny's serves breakfast for dinner, but dessert for breakfast? The dessert choices were pie alamode, chocolate-chip pancakes, or fruit. Fruit! Where'd that come from? None of us had saved room for dessert.

After our ride briefing, we took the obligatory, last day, group picture and then headed out, walking our tandem to the bottom of the hill. This was a wise choice because of the loose gravel and steepness of the hill. So we took off riding again, this time on rolling hills into New York State on the southwest corner of Vermont. New York was definitely not as pretty a state as Vermont. The first thing we noticed were advertising signs everywhere blocking the scenery. We weren't even aware that Vermont had almost no roadside signs until we went into New York. We biked along to the town of Cambridge, NY where the others joined us and we ate lunch. Sally and I split a light tuna salad sandwich and probably the best iced mocha decaf we had ever had. It was actually a frappe, but it sure was good. Since we had to drive to Brattleboro that evening for a presentation Sally was giving to a paralegal group, we told the others we would see them later. Daring to ask Saunie, Saunie, Saunie about the terrain the rest of the way back, we were told there was a long challenging uphill the rest of the way.

She was wrong one more time. The terrain was slightly uphill, but the road was smooth and we cranked it up. We cruised at twenty plus mph most of the way and were making good time. Besides, there was nothing more to see in New York anyway. We re-entered Vermont and were now just trying to burn up calories so we could eat what we hadn't eaten from the menu the night before. I was craving a steak. Biking on a river road adjacent to the Battenkill River, we passed by Norman Rockwell's home at the outskirts of Arlington. We slowed when we went through the covered bridge that lead away from the house, entered the main highway, and started to hammer again. Patrick passed us immediately after the bridge, pulled to a stop about a quarter of a mile ahead, got out of the van, and was trying to tell us something. We had a head of steam up so I gave him the "we're okay" wave and blew on by. He actually tried running along side of us for about twenty feet (like something from a keystone cop movie), but I never heard what he was saying (did I mention I don't hear so good). I knew we were heading in the right direction and didn't want to stop.

Later he said he wanted to take our picture as we passed through the covered bridge, but he underestimated our speed on the tandem and didn't get to the bridge before we did. I think this day we averaged more than nine miles per hour over the forty-three mile course, but some of it was in New York, not Vermont.

Dinner that night was soooo good, especially when it came soooo late. We didn't get back from Brattleboro until a little after eight o'clock, but they all waited for us and I scarfed down a big juicy steak. I finished all of my seven courses since I bike to eat. Charlotte and John didn't eat with us since she had gotten sick with John's illness and John was still not feeling well. They both rode that day and I have to give credit to John for riding up the hill to the inn. It was a steep one. Sally and I tried it, but our thighs were burning from a fast ride. We had to push the tandem up the hill and that caused some minor back spasms for me. Since chocolate is a cure for my back spasms, I had the chocolate cheesecake for dessert. Because of my poor hearing, I thought the waitress had said zucchini cake. This provided some amusement for the less hearing impaired at our table. My back spasms, of course, went away after the cheesecake.

Day Five

The last day of our ride, Alex and Allison left early in their car to try to make it to Cape Cod before sunset, so they did not ride. John and Charlotte still were not feeling the best, so it was just Cap'n Johnnye and Stoker Sally for the last day's ride. Of course breakfast was the same as before, too much to eat, but I tried. I warmed up with one of the pecan-maple bars I had found in my pocket from the day before. No one could eat the sticky buns so they wrapped them up for later. Saunie, Saunie, Saunie was not riding, but she did order the ooey-gooey eggs. They were fried eggs smothered in Vermont cheese and loaded with calories. I couldn't bear to watch her to see if she had eaten it all. Besides, I was engulfed in an omelet the size of Kansas with a flood of cheese oozing out of the sides and chunks of ham the size of footballs. I had also ordered a side of Canadian bacon knowing it must be fresh since Vermont is close to the Canadian border.

Patrick took our car back to Manchester where the first day's ride had started and the last day's ride ends. There was one option on this ride to make the total eighteen miles so we decided to do it. The weather was perfect and our ride took us up on another tree-lined road looking down into the valley to the west. We took it easy not wanting the ride or the trip to end. Since our maximum speed thus far had only been thirty-eight and a half, I saw a chance to up it a bit on a long downhill straightaway going under State Route Seven. With Sally screaming for her life (make fun of me and my zucchini cake will you), I hauled in the anchor and let 'er rip. She wouldn't tell me how fast we were going until we hit the bottom of the hill and slowed down. When she said forty-five and a half, I knew we could have hit fifty if we could have gotten a little more aerodynamic. To cut down on the wind resistance, she would have had to close her mouth instead of yelling obscenities at me.

Well, back at the Manchester Highlands Inn, we cleaned up, got our civvies on, said goodbye to Saunie, Saunie, Saunie and Patrick (Sally, the emotional one, did her little crying bit), and got all our stuff together to depart. It was a bit sad, making and leaving friends, ending a terrific trip, and knowing we probably would not ride with Bike Vermont again next year for the fifth time in a row (well maybe).

We bought property in Shaftsbury last year and were planning a move to Vermont in the spring of 2000 (sooner if we could win the Lotto). I wonder if our bike computer is year 2000 compliant? To seal our promise to return, we left our helmets and Bike Vermont water bottles sitting on the chairs overlooking our pond on our property in Shaftsbury.

By the way, we didn't gain an ounce. Bike to eat.

Why I'm The Rev.
Or
Life Is Too Short
To Have Only One Title

For now, my full title is The Honorable Reverend Dr. Cap'n St. Johnnye, SS, PE, EE, IE, EA, Director of Traffic, LSMFT all of which are legit except for the LSMFT. Isn't that set of titles a whole lot better than just plain ol' Mr.? Well, maybe not, but let me explain anyway.

When I was working for the Indian Health Service, DHHS, in Dallas, someone had placed copies of pages from the Bible in my inbox almost daily. I had not gone to church in at least fifteen years and openly professed no religious affiliation. I had been a Catholic before I quit going to church because of a silly reason. My wife and I had attended mass on the Saturday before Easter. Saturday vigil mass to fulfill the Catholic obligation of going to church on Sunday was a relatively new concept in the early 70s, and one well received by my wife and me. Saturday vigil mass meant that we would miss the comedy variety show, Hee Haw, but it also meant that we could sleep in on Sunday and for one day I could skip the daily shaving ritual.

When mass was over on that one Holy Saturday back in 1973, the priest turned to the congregation and after the blessing, stated, "You know this doesn't count. You must still attend mass tomorrow morning."

"What does he mean, it doesn't count?" I asked my wife on the way back to our apartment.

"I guess Saturday mass before Easter doesn't fulfill our Easter Sunday obligation," she replied.

"But, going to mass must count for something, no matter when you go," I countered.

We missed mass the next morning, and every week for the next 32 years. My wife, I felt, was a "reluctant" Catholic anyway, only going to mass because I wanted to. So when I suggested we find something to do on Saturday night that "counted" like watching Hee Haw, I received no argument from her.

When we got to the Bible Belt country in Dallas by way of New Jersey, Corpus Christi, and Okinawa, Japan, we were surrounded by a large population of religious people, mostly Southern Baptists, whom I dubbed with the acronym SOBs. After several conversations with my fellow workers about religion and my statements that I had doubts about the existence of any God, I started getting the "Bibles for Dummies" treatment. To my statements about a lack of any belief in God, I had added, "...but, if there was one, She would be a black woman with a sense of humor."

It didn't matter that I would cross out He and put She and make other pertinent changes on the Bible pages that began to appear in my inbox and then stick them in my outbox, the lessons just kept coming. I guess they were trying to "save" me.

It was after about a year of this "convert the heathen" treatment that I stumbled upon what I thought was a solution. The internet was in its infancy, but I was state-of-the-art with my own PC at home, one that I had built from a Heathkit. While probing around online, I stumbled on a place, Universal Life Church (ULC), where I could buy a "Ministry-in-a-box" kit for only $39.99. For another $10, they would throw in a doctorate of divinity. I must have gotten in on the ground floor, because the same kit now costs $139.99.

But wait, there's more. For a limited time only, if I acted now, I would also get sainthood.

When my Ministry-in-a-box came, I made a copy of my doctorate of divinity and appointment as reverend in the ULC and posted it on the wall of my cubicle. This worked. The Bible excerpts quit showing up in my inbox. It was as if whoever was trying to convert me gave up, realizing that I was a hard case, beyond salvation, and probably was going to hell no matter what they attempted.

Twenty years later, I registered as a minister and was legally able to solemnize a wedding (sodomize was what I called it). Shortly thereafter, I performed my first wedding ceremony and two years later, my second one. So, I am legally a reverend with all due rights and privileges (if I want them).

If you have read my submarine book, *Fairy Tales and Sea Stories*, you would know that two of my Navy buddies had given me the title of Cap'n, short for Captain. I don't know where they got it other than the skipper of the boat and I were the only two on our sub who had actually gone to the Naval Academy. He graduated and worked his way up to the rank of captain. I quit and worked my way back down to deck hand and bottle washer. Nonetheless, I added the title, Cap'n, to my full name. I was now the Reverend Doctor Cap'n St. Johnny.

Shortly after my divorce, I met a woman online who had a cat named Charlye. I thought that was an unusual way to spell Charley, so I wrote my first Children's book under the name of Cap'n Johnnye, adding an "e" to the end of Johnny in honor of her cat, Charlye. This changed my title slightly.

I was getting bored with the same Reverend Doctor Cap'n St. Johnnye, so I started looking for more ways to add to my name as from the book, *The Peter Principle*, where one of the results from a Lateral Arabesque was the addition of more meaningless job titles. Up until then, I had been overlooking the fact that I did have two degrees, one as an electrical engineer, EE, and a masters in industrial engineering, IE. In addition, I have a professional engineering license, PE, and am a licensed energy auditor, EA, both of which were earned while living in Texas. Finally, from my Navy days, I qualified in the submarine service which gave me the designation SS. These five facts allowed me to be the Reverend Doctor Cap'n St. Johnnye, SS, PE, EE, IE, EA.
This still was not enough.

I had been a volunteer with the monthly Kiwanis food distribution and worked my way up to being in charge, so to speak, of the drive-through area where the food is placed into the cars. I arrive early in the morning, set up the barricades and more or less direct the traffic into and out of the loading zones. So I call myself the Director of Traffic, which I added to the end of the engineering titles.

Next, I saw an opportunity to be a judge at the annual science fair with the local college. I thought that being a judge would allow me to add "The Honorable" to the beginning of my name. When the judging was over, I added it.

So now, my full title is The Honorable Reverend Dr. Cap'n St. Johnnye, SS, PE, EE, IE, EA, Director of Traffic. As a joke, I added the LSMFT to the very end. Those who grew up in the 50s and 60s might remember the cigarette ads which were so prevalent. One of those was for Lucky Strike cigarettes with the letters LSMFT on the packaging. It stands for Lucky Strike Means Fine Tobacco, or if you had been a member of the generation who grew up in early 1900's, it meant Lord Save Me From Taft, who was the 27th President from 1909 to 1913.

That is my full title for now, but wait, there's more.

If I become a member of The Knights of Columbus and work my way up far enough, I can add "Sir," which I think fits nicely between Dr. and Cap'n. I am still looking for other ways to add to my titles, so if you have any ideas, please send them to me. Life is too short to have only one title.

How To Get A Lincoln Town Car Stuck In The Mud

"This was the car that had to be towed in," I told the PYT behind the Budget Rental Car counter.

"Oh, I'm so sorry," she replied, with a look of concern on her sweet innocent-looking face. "Allow me to comp the rental cost? Here, there is no charge for the car." She handed me back the receipt stamped 'no cost to customer.'

I was so shocked I didn't respond. Besides, I had a flight to catch so I scurried away, receipt in hand. It was Gerry's credit card anyway, and it wasn't because the car was disabled that we had to call for a tow, although the transmission was probably ruined. Let me explain.

It was a dark and stormy night!

Well, okay, it wasn't, but it was a cold, early spring morning in Albuquerque, New Mexico. I met Gerry for the free breakfast at the motel on the north end of town on Alameda Street, just off Route 25. The motel was our favorite place to stay whenever we came to Albuquerque to do business with the Indian Health Service area office. We liked the motel because of the free manager's social, which included free booze – wine for me and "watch and scotter" for Gerry (he always pronounced scotch and water that way which masked his slurred pronunciation a few drinks later). Don, the area office representative, always joined us and ordered a Bloody Mary or three, or four, or....

We were on per diem, which was a government euphemism for spending your own money. This was because the feds didn't give us enough to live on. So, we took advantage of the places that provided free drinks and snacks at the manager's social in the evening and free breakfast each morning. That would ensure that we had enough per diem left over to buy lunch and dinner, occasionally.

Even though our business was in Dulce that day, some three and a half hours to the north, we stayed in Albuquerque. By staying in Albuquerque, we would spend seven hours of driving the next day for a one-hour meeting, and we would make damn sure to get back in time for the manager's social that night. We could have stayed in Santa Fe or Taos and slept a little later, but those towns were more expensive and no free anything. The extra money it cost to stay in either Santa Fe or Taos would have had to have come from our pockets. Also, staying in Albuquerque gave Don, who lived and worked in Albuquerque, a chance to join us for breakfast, ride with us to the meeting, and join us for social hour back at the motel. We were always considerate of the needs of others.

I had only stayed in Santa Fe once and Taos once and had found the hotels there lacking in one way or another. Gerry had once talked me into staying at a quaint, picturesque hotel on the south end of Santa Fe. By quaint, he meant tiny. It had a bedroom and bathroom like other motels, but the bed had to be crawled into from the foot since it was sandwiched between two walls and there were no sides to sidle up to. How the maid was able to change the sheets without crawling all over the bed was a mystery in itself. I had had enough of a challenge just figuring out how to use the bathroom.

To say that the bathroom was tiny would have been an understatement. While sitting on the toilet, I was able to brush my teeth in the sink at the same time without having to stretch. The shower was so small—how small was it? It was so small; I had to decide which side of my body I wanted to wash first, then get out, turn around, and crab walk back in to wash the other side. I have to admit that the walls of the quaint hotel were like the walls of the Alamo, which are some twelve feet thick, but I'm not into architecture, especially when staying at a hotel that ate into my per diem allowance, leaving no money for food.

So, I had had it with staying at quaint, little places away from the freebees and comforts of a telephone, TV, and turn-around-in shower stall and insisted that we stay in Albuquerque with its freebies.

"I have an emergency at home," Gerry said, halfway through breakfast. "You'll have to go with Don to the meeting using my rental car. I have a shuttle taking me to the airport in a half an hour."

"Oh," was all I said. I didn't ask what the emergency was. In addition to being someone I supervised, I also considered Gerry a friend. If he wanted me to know what the emergency was, he would have told me, so I didn't say anything else. We had worked closely on the planning of the renovation project, and having been a project manager myself for umpteen years before getting my promotion to branch chief, I knew what had to be done.

Before becoming a supervisor, I had done most of my project management with the Phoenix area office, a different branch from the one I was now supervising. Having been promoted to branch chief just a few months earlier, I was now the supervisor of the people who did projects for the Albuquerque area. This trip was an excuse to observe those whom I supervised and to show the area office that we really cared about their projects. Going on a supervising trip also got me away from the office for awhile. Project management was fun; supervision was boring, but paid better.

"Here are the keys to the car," Gerry said. "It's the gray Town Car parked in front."

"Town Car?" I said in disbelief. Our strict instructions were to rent the cheapest vehicle available, first to save taxpayer money, and second, to avoid giving the impression that we were wasting the area's budget money (the area office ultimately paid for our trips with project money). Occasionally I would get a free upgrade from sub-compact to a larger car, but only because the cheaper one was not available. I knew a Lincoln was way above the "cheapest car possible" mandate.

"Yes," Gerry explained. "I got a free upgrade because I come here so often and was able to use one of my free coupons."

Those coupons were supposed to be turned in along with frequent flyer points so the government could stuff them in a desk somewhere and let them expire. We all knew this is what happened to the coupons if we turned them in, so we used them as often as we could get away with it.

I didn't say anything else as I pocketed the keys. During this conversation, Don never looked up from his scrambled eggs, hash browns, and coffee. Don was in uniform and a member of the commissioned corps. The uniform had been styled after the Navy officer's uniform with navy blue pants, coat, and tie with a white shirt and shiny black shoes. On his sleeve were the gold bars of a lieutenant.

Don was a Native American, a really nice guy, and a golden gloves champ. One of the first trips I took with him and Gerry was to the Acoma Pueblo to the west of Albuquerque. Don knew most of the back roads and was our guide to the more hard-to-get-to destinations. On that trip to the Pueblo, it was an overcast day with low temperatures and high humidity. As we drove through one canyon, we came upon a densely forested hill to our right with the mist picturesquely clinging to the tops of the trees.

"The hills are on fire!" Don declared from the rear seat. "We better find a phone and call it in."

This was before the omnipresent cell phone. Later when I did get a cell phone, because of a lack of towers on reservations, it was basically useless in the areas we frequented.

After hearing Don's "the hills are on fire" comment, Gerry, who was driving, looked in the rear view mirror at Don, and then at me in the passenger seat. I turned around to look at Don who was as serious as I had ever seen him.

"That's a fog bank," Gerry said.

"Oh," Don responded and turned a deeper shade of red than his natural color.

"And the army used to use you guys as guides in the 1800s?" I asked.

Gerry laughed at this and almost ran us off the road.

"You were serious?" Gerry asked of Don.

"Well, it could have been a fire," Don protested, and just stared out of the window avoiding further eye contact with either of us. After that, we shared the story at every social hour we could, which got a lot of laughs at poor Don's expense.

"We'll leave right after we finish eating, before the hills catch on fire." I announced to Don, who looked up from his chow, long enough to acknowledge my statement and give me a dirty look.

"I put all the documents in the Town Car," Gerry said after he had nearly choked on the last of his coffee over my comment about the hills.

"I'll meet you out front in five," I said to Don. "I want to go back to my room and get my jacket."

Don nodded and I got up to leave.

"Have a good trip back," I said to Gerry. "I hope everything turns out okay."

"Thanks," he said, his thoughts far away. "I appreciate your taking over for me today."

"I don't mind," I lied. I was a bit perturbed, but what else could I do. The project was important to the tribe and there were a lot of people waiting for our discussion and short presentation. We were the guys who were supposed to have all the answers.

I had only been to Dulce once before, and the project manager I was with, not Gerry, had been there several times and knew a back way that bypassed Santa Fe. Going to Santa Fe and then north through Chama was the longer way, but it used major roads. I remembered that his shortcut had taken us through a town called Cuba. I also remembered that there were some rather large symbolic teepees that we had passed, but couldn't remember where they were. My one trip to Dulce was a long time ago and I had been a passenger taking in the raw beauty of the Jicarilla-Apache Indian Reservation and other sites along the way instead of making mental notes of the roads we had taken. I did remember that the shortcut roads were paved, but definitely not major thoroughfares.

Driving around on the Indian Reservations required the skills of a good scout. The roads were poorly marked, if at all. All of the project managers in the office navigated by landmarks. Directions to strangers were also given by such directions as… "drive south on I-10, exit at the Sacaton Trading Post, head south about four miles, and turn right at the three saguaro cacti. A lot of the existing places we went to were hospitals, so it was easy to get there by following the blue and white "H" direction signs.

When I was project manager at the new Sacaton Hospital in Sacaton, Arizona, I knew the route by heart having had to go there twice a month for almost two years. When I gave directions, however, it was difficult to describe how to get there through the desolate desert area south of Phoenix, until one tragic day. A Native American was riding his pinto pony along the main route to the hospital when he was struck and killed by a car right at the critical, unmarked turnoff to the new construction site. When I passed by the site on my bi-monthly trip to inspect the construction progress, I saw the chalked crime-scene outline of where the poor man had died in the middle of the intersection, horse and all. The grisly chalked outline on the road of a man on horseback was still there the next time I passed by, so now I had a more definitive marker to direct visitors to the site.

"Turn left at the body outlines," I would say.

"Huh?" was the usual response and then I would explain.

This worked for about six months, until the outlines faded in the blazing desert sun and the annual rain storm. I lost my marker for a couple of winter months until I noticed two reservation dogs had met the same fate as the man on horseback. This time, there were no outlines of the bodies, but the two dead dogs were there instead. The carcasses remained throughout the entire summer months (in Phoenix this was April to November). They lay along the side of the road, flattened from being run over numerous times, but there they remained plastered to the asphalt to mark the turnoff to the construction site.

"Turn left at the two-dead dogs," I instructed.

"Huh?"

I used this same method of direction giving where we had lived in the rental house affectionately nicknamed Yellow Hell in South Shaftsbury, Vermont. As on the reservations, there are few signs in rural Vermont, so directions had to be given by landmarks. While going home one day, I was traveling north on 7A into South Shaftsbury, and right before Cleveland Avenue, the turnoff to Yellow Hell, I noticed a skunk had been hit and left to die by the side of the road. The stench was excruciating.

After a few days the smell dissipated, but the remains of the skunk had stained the road and were still there. I was reminded of the "two dead dogs" in Sacaton. A couple of days later, while going south on 7A, I was treated to, not the usual rank smell of fried food from Paulen's convenience store (a place where every entrée was fried in rancid oil), but to the savory aroma of another skunk, this one on the way into South Shaftsbury from the North. Now I could direct visitors to our little rental house much the same way I directed visitors to the Sacaton Hospital. "From the south, turn left at the dead skunk onto Cleveland Street and then left onto Holiday Drive. From the north, turn left at the intersection after the dead skunk and then left onto Cleveland Street....

"Huh?"

I could have done that until someone or something removed the two skunks.

I got to the Town Car before Don and grabbed the map that was provided by the Budget Rental Car company and made a mental note of the turn-off of I-25 toward the northwest at Bernalillo about a third of the way to Santa Fe. I located the town of Cuba on Route 550 and the town of Dulce due north of Cuba. The rental car map showed a road skirting the reservation and connecting the two towns.

This must be the way, I thought. *Besides, I've got Don with me and he must know the shortcut.* Don showed up a couple of minutes later carrying a cup of coffee that he had gotten free from the motel dining room.

"Ready?" I said as he got in.

"Ready," he replied.

"We're taking the shortcut and by-passing Santa Fe," I announced, pointing to the roads on the map.

"I don't know that way," Don responded.

Great, I thought. *He's the area representative and we're going to his meeting with his project managers on a trip where I was just supposed to observe, and he doesn't know the way.*

With that, we headed north out of Albuquerque. By the time we had gotten to Bernalillo, about 10 miles north of Albuquerque, Don was leaning against the passenger side door with his eyes closed. I turned northwest on Route 550 toward Cuba some 35 miles away. We passed through the Santa Ana Indian reservation with its arroyos, dry gulches, and very few trees. Less than a half hour later we passed Cuba and I thought the turn-off was just up the road. I came to a place to turn north, but there were no teepees. I turned onto the road and headed north.

They must have taken the teepees down, I thought.

A few miles up the road I saw a marker which indicated Route 96. I grabbed for the rental-car-company road map and flipped it around until I found Cuba. Don was still crapped out against the door with his head resting between the door and the seat headrest.

I noticed on the map that the road I was really supposed to turn right on was Route 537 on the Jicarilla Apache Indian Reservation about 12 miles further from Cuba than where I had turned. The map indicated that this road, Route 96, was paved all the way to Route 84 which is the main road between Santa Fe and Dulce, our destination.

What the heck, I thought. *I've bypassed Santa Fe, which was my goal, and this road is paved and smooth.*

I forged ahead, but came to the intersection of 112 and 96, the map indicated 96 went due east, back toward 84 and 112 would take us further north to 84. Route 112 was paved so I kept heading north. I set the cruise control on 55.

Ten miles later, we rounded a bend to the right with a stand of small trees blocking the line of sight. I glanced at Don, still curled up against the door. When I looked up again, the road suddenly turned to dirt. It was hard packed, and still frozen over as it was shaded from the morning sun by the trees. I was about to brake with the intention of turning around, when we passed over the frozen part and hit the ruts which had been carved out by the thawing mud and others who had gone before me.

The Lincoln made a bump, bump sound and jarred Don out of his slumbering state.

"What's that," he asked. "Where are we?"

"I don't know," I said, with eyes as wide as an owl's on a moonlit night. "We just hit mud and deep ruts. I can't turn around and I can't stop or we'll get stuck."

Don was alert now and I was driving with my chin almost resting on the steering wheel. I was holding on tightly, but the road was doing the guiding as the wheels were caught in the ruts like a train on a track. The transmission and undercarriage were plowing the center of the road consisting rock and of clumps of dirt.

"We'll make it," I said, with very little confidence in my voice. "As long as we don't stop and it doesn't get any worse, we'll make it."

I checked the angle of the sun to see if its melting effects would make the road worse. Don grabbed the map and I pointed to the road that we had taken a few miles back.

"That's the road we're on, and the map indicates that it's paved."

"Obviously in error," Don replied.

I did not respond. I just stared unblinkingly straight ahead.

"Oh shit!" I said. "There's a boulder in the road, right in the middle."

I was able to steer a little to the right and the Lincoln rode up a little higher on the sides of the rutted road. Two loud bangs sounded as the Town Car jumped a little when the transmission and differential bounced over the rock. I glanced in the rear-view mirror and saw sprays of mud whipping up on the back window as the wheels settled back into the center of the grooves.

"How far have we gone?" Don asked.

"We passed a sign that said Llaves about five minutes before we hit the dirt," I said.

He rechecked the map.

"It looks like we have about eight or ten more miles to go before we get to 84," Don said.

"We'll make it, we'll make it," I replied, trying to convince myself.

But at the top of a small rise, my heart sank. There was a pickup truck right in the middle of the road. There was no going around it as the ruts here were as deep as the axles. There also was no place to go on either side had we been able to get out of the ruts.

"There's a hunter," Don said, glancing to the left of the truck.

A man with a rifle was standing about fifty feet from the truck staring over the next rise. I slowed hoping that he could get back to his truck before we had to stop. He noticed us and headed back to his truck, but was in no hurry. I had to stop when I got to within twenty feet of the truck.

"We're screwed" I said, and slumped my head down on the steering wheel.

The man got back to his truck and laid his rifle in the bed of the pickup. He got in, started the truck and pulled slowly away. I gave the Lincoln some gas and we moved, just a little before the wheels started spinning. It was front-wheel drive, but what we needed was four-wheels to dig us out of here. I tried to accelerate a little harder, but all I succeeded in doing was flinging mud up onto the hood and roof of the car.

The man in the pickup stopped, got out and walked back to us. I rolled down the window to talk to him.

"What' ja doin' up here?" he asked.

"We made a wrong turn," I said. "We would have been all right if we hadn't had to stop."

I knew it wasn't any good to switch the blame from me to him, but he could have pulled off the road to do his hunting. His truck was not four-wheel drive, but it rode a lot higher than the Town Car and did not drag on in the center of the road.

"Ya got a chain?"

What did he think this was a tow truck? I thought.

Don and I got out of the car to asses the situation.

"No" I said. "This is a rental car."

"I've got a chain back at the camp," he offered. "I can come back and tow ya out."

I was walking on the mud and gaining about an inch in height with every step. The thawing mud was like the clay in Texas which stuck to the bottom of shoes like chewing gum. Don was in his uniform shiny dress military shoes and was having the same problem. At least he was in the blue winter uniform and not his summer whites. I was going to see if the hunter could get his truck behind us and push us out, but if he damaged the rental car, I would be liable, or at least the government would have to pay. Since this was off-road use and in violation of the rental agreement, I would have a real fight with the rental car company, my insurance, and the government.

Damn, that Gerry, I thought.

Only it wasn't his fault. I chose this route.

"Let's try and push it out," Don said.

"It's worth a try. If I we can just get it moving a little we'll be all right." I said, but was thinking that the effort would be futile.

I got back in the car while Don and the hunter got behind the Lincoln. I gunned the car as they pushed and lifted, but the front wheels just spun, flinging more mud up onto the hood and roof. A little more gunning and wheel spinning and I could smell it. From past experience of working in an auto repair shop, I knew the odor to be that of burning transmission fluid. Smoke started to seep out of the engine compartment.

"That's it!" I exclaimed.

The car had not moved at all. The undercarriage was resting on the center of the road. I grabbed the lever under the dashboard and popped the hood. Don, with mud all over his uniform came around and opened the hood. I stepped out of the car and saw what he was looking at. There was no fire, but mud was packed up on top of the engine as if we were trying to bury it. The blue-gray smoke was lessening, but it was obvious the transmission was about shot.

"Can you give us a ride to Chama, and I'll call a wrecker?" I asked hopefully.

"Sure" the hunter said.

I gathered up the documents that we would need noticing that we had tracked a considerable amount of mud inside the car. I didn't think that anyone would steal the Lincoln, but someone might cause further damage to it if they thought that it was abandoned, so I locked it. At least that way if someone did damage it, I could say that I diligently locked all the doors. Don and I piled into the pickup and we pulled away silently. We passed a reservoir on the left and less than a mile away from the Lincoln the road turned to asphalt pavement again.

"All we had to do was make it this far," I said.

We told the hunter what had happened and why we were in Indian Country. He was a member of the Jicarilla Apaches and was out hunting deer around the reservoir.

He dropped us off at a restaurant in Chama and I called a wrecker company.

"Bring a big tow truck," I said with emphasis on big.

I then called the people who were waiting for us in Dulce. They said they still wanted the meeting and would bring everyone to the restaurant. I checked with the owner of the restaurant and he was happy to accommodate us, so I told them to come on. Dulce was only about

15 miles away, so Don and I ordered coffee and spread the drawings out on a large table.

"We'll have to call a cab to get us back to Albuquerque," I sad to Don. "I hope there's one in Santa Fe. There goes my per diem."

While waiting for the team to arrive, Don and I used the time to clean up, especially Don, whose uniform and shoes were mud caked. He didn't seem to care even though his dry cleaning bill would be a little higher this month. The Commissioned Corps must have been giving him an allowance for uniform maintenance.

The participants from the clinic in Dulce arrived and we explained what had happened. About halfway through the presentation, a man came in from the wrecker service.

"How far up in there are ya?" he asked.

He must have been familiar with the road and pulled others out of there before.

"About a mile from the end of the paved road, on this end," I said.

"Ya did good to get that far if ya came in from the south end," he said.

"We would have made it all the way had there not been a truck in the way," I said. I hope you brought a big tow truck, because it's a Lincoln Town Car and it's stuck pretty good."

"Oh, yeah," he said, nodding towards the parking lot and sounding unconcerned.

"I glanced through the window and saw that he was right. It was an all wheel dually, the kind used to tow large 18 wheelers.

When the tow truck driver had left, we resumed our meeting.

"All we have to do now is find a way back to Albuquerque," I said when the session was ended.

"One of the nurses commutes back and forth to Albuquerque," one of the doctors intoned matter-of-factly. "Let me see if she's still at the clinic."

Using the phone at the counter, he made a quick call to the clinic and came back smiling.

"She's on her way," he said.

Finally, a bit of luck, I thought.

Apologizing for the meeting starting later than scheduled, we said our goodbyes to our clients. They didn't seem to care about the delay, as events happened slower on the reservation. They were just glad to have their badly needed renovation project moving forward. Taking in the nice crisp spring air, we waited for our ride outside. We only had to wait about ten minutes and just before she came we saw the tow truck with the Town Car in tow pull into a gas station across the street. Covered in dried mud, it looked like it was painted brown instead black.

Pulling in to pick us up, the nurse did not have to ask if we were the ones needing a ride back to Albuquerque. She was quite attractive, and talking to her on the way back was a pleasant experience. Of course we told her the entire story. She went back through Santa Fe, which would be my path of travel if I ever had to drive back this way again.

About ten minutes out of Albuquerque, I checked my watch.

"Don, guess what?" I asked.

"What," he said, a little miffed that I had interrupted his conversation with the pretty nurse.

Don was single, and I was married, but I could still admire one of the opposite sex.

"We're going to make happy hour," I informed him, then added directing my question to the nurse. "Would you like to join us?"

"No," she said. "I have to get back to my place and feed my cat, but thanks for asking."

The happy hour snacks and drinks were enough for me, and I had no transportation to go out for dinner so I was in for the night. I said goodbye to Don as he left in his car which he had parked at the motel that morning. The hotel had a shuttle service which I would take to the airport in the morning, where I returned the keys to the Budget counter at the airport.

Epilog

"What's this extra charge for cleaning on the bill for the car in Albuquerque?" Gerry asked, tossing the bill down on my desk.

Since he had been on personal leave since I had come back from Albuquerque and until now, I hadn't seen him since we had parted ways in the hotel in Albuquerque, he didn't know the story.

"I returned it a little dirty," I said, smiling sheepishly.

"A little?" he said. "How about $200 worth of a little."

Even though I was his supervisor, he felt comfortable enough to confront me with this obvious hit on his per diem. After I explained, and added the fact that I had only been to Chama once before and really didn't know the way, he calmed down. There were no other charges such as: towing, transmission repair, body repair, and repainting, which amazed me.

We took the bill to the financial guru (called the comptroller in government lingo) that handled all of our reimbursable expenses and rental car charges. Blaming the whole thing on the map that the rental car company had provided, which I had kept for evidence, he was able to convince Budget to drop the cleaning charge. After all, we did do a lot of business with them.

I still don't know what the personal business was that kept Gerry from driving that day.

The next story is a sequel to this one and could have occurred the night that we had returned from Chama.

UVULA

Happy hour at the hotel meant we would be having hydraulic sandwiches for dinner. A hydraulic sandwich is anything liquid containing alcohol that can be placed in a glass container. Sort of like pastrami on rye, only it's booze in a bottle or glass. Whenever a guest checked into the hotel where we stayed, coupons for happy hour drinks were distributed. The hotel never checked to whom they had given the coupons so we could always go back to the front desk and get more.

"Someone told me that you had drink coupons for hotel guests," was the line we had practiced.

"Yes, sir, we do," the clerk said.

"Well, I didn't get any," we would say with raised eyebrows.

"I'm so sorry," the clerk would say. "Here are a couple of extras for being so patient."

When we came back from our business meetings later in the day, there was usually a new night clerk on duty, so we launched into the same routine.

"Someone told me that…"

In addition to our "I didn't get any" routine, some of the people in our office did not drink, so they would give us their coupons. I was the supervisor, so a little brown-nosing was always nice to try. My favorite drinking partner, Gerry, and I had so many accumulated coupons that we could drink for a month without paying anything and invite all of our local contacts too. Sometimes we would go out to eat after happy hour, but not usually.

One of the "not usually" times I stumbled back to my room around 8:00 to retire for the night. Eight o'clock was not unusual since my biological clock was on Texas time, which was an hour later than Albuquerque time. In Texas I was used to going to bed at 10:00 anyway. After brushing my teeth, I got into bed and decided to see

158

what was on the cable. I turned on the TV and channel surfed until I got to what looked like an interesting program on the surgery channel. I could blame it on my poor hearing, or the alcohol, but most likely it was a combination of both, for what I heard the surgeon say was '...and now we take hold of the vulva and make a small incision like this.' I couldn't believe I was so lucky to be able to watch what I thought was as close to porn as I could get for free. I had never seen one up close with all the lights shining directly on it and with it spread out like that.

I watched intently for almost an hour, waiting for the moment when the camera would back out and expose the entire groin area. And don't they have to shave for an operation like that? I was not going to miss this even though I had to piss badly and needed to get some sleep.

After some snipping and suturing and some other procedural explanations, which I didn't understand, the surgeon said 'That's about all for this operation,' and the camera started its slow retreat. Suddenly there appeared a set of blurry white objects, first on the top, and then on the bottom of the screen. As the camera retreated further, the objects came into focus. They were teeth. I didn't know the vulva had teeth. I had always heard horror stories about how things could be inserted in the vagina which would shred a penis when it was inserted, but teeth.

Time and the shock of seeing teeth where I thought the vulva was, sobered me up considerably. As the surgeon said 'that's the way we repair a cleft pallet,' I realized I mistook vulva for uvula. I spent nearly 45 minutes watching a stinking program about a mouth operation hoping to catch a glimpse of a woman's crotch. I changed channels faster than as if I had turned to a Mexican station on the radio. From now on I vowed to turn on the closed captioning or go to my room sober (fat chance that).

What To Do With Road Kill

Other than the obvious of opening up a mobile, fast food stand on the side of the road, what could you do with road kill?

This past summer had been a particularly lethal one for the local fauna on the roads leading out of my hometown of Alliance, Ohio. While riding my bicycle south of town on busy Union Avenue, our biking group passed several unfortunate creatures of varying types. There were, listed in order of frequency: raccoons, possums, squirrels, groundhogs (AKA woodchucks, AKA marmots, AKA whistle-pigs), skunks, assorted birds, cats, and an occasional dog.

As bikers we have to be on the lookout for these obstacles as when hit on a bicycle and still relatively fresh, they can cause loss of control and possibly an accident. When not as fresh but still moist, in addition to causing a gag reflex when a cyclist is breathing heavily, they can be a flavor enhancer. I mean flavor enhancer in the sense that some of the ooze can be thrown back and up by the front wheel onto our water bottles. The rear wheel can also throw back entrails onto the biker behind you or, if particularly sticky, all the way up onto the back of your Tour-de-France racing jersey. While the stuck-to-your-back entrails dried in the mid-morning sun they would begin to resemble a road map of the French Alps. By the time you reached the stop-over lunch break eating establishment, you might elicit some comments from the person behind you such as, "My, is that a map of this years Marseilles to Bordeaux bike race?"

Our usual daily routes passed by the same carcasses sometimes every day, which allowed us to observe the changes from fresh kill, to balloon bulge, to crow bait, to road taco, and to the final stage, sail-cat. As described in the *Bikers Handbook of Unusual Scenic Wonders*, fresh kill is that which had been laid out the night before and has various body parts exposed to the outside world. At this point it could be taken to the closest Mexican restaurant and exchanged for a coupon for a free road-kill burrito with purchase of one margarita the size of a small fish bowl.

Balloon bulge is described as that mostly intact carcass that had been affected by the hot summer sun. It is now in danger of floating away like the Goodyear blimp, but is held fast by strands of ooze that, during the night, had seeped out of both end orifices, dried, and attached themselves to the pavement like land lines that hold a ship to a dock.

Crow bait is just that. The ever increasing pressure of expanding gasses caused the critter to burst spewing forth a colorful, edible version of a Picasso painting. Various scavenger birds had discovered the easy meal and are brave enough to venture to the side of the road to pick and choose from a warm smorgasbord. However, they must be wary of passing eighteen-wheelers so that the suction created by the large vehicles does not make out of the not-too-quick birds, an instant road taco themselves.

The road taco stage is where the sun has baked, the birds have picked, and passing time has reduced the remains to a still colorful and still identifiable thin pancake resembling what Don Pancho's Restaurant and Taqueria sells three for five dollars on Tuesday evening.

Then finally the last stage, that of sail cat. This usually occurs at the end of summer when the heat, birds, and passing road traffic have reduced the now unidentifiable creature to an infinitesimally thin mass of flattened hide and exposed sun-bleached bones. The animal wafer is stuck to the pavement in an oblong shape with the tail leading away from the main mess. At this time, grabbing hold of the tail and lifting up results in a sound like two pieces of Velcro being pulled apart until the last of it comes up with a snap. The pasteboard thin sail cat can now be flung like a Frisbee across the adjoining field coming to rest where it will become fertilizer for next year's corn harvest.

Then, next riding season, it will start all over again.

The following story is dedicated to the memory or Jim Heddleson and all the veterans of WW II, including my father who had to fight in the big one. I came to know Jim through a mutual friend who introduced us for the purpose of my ghost writing his story. He had been shot down in France behind enemy lines while working for the Office of Strategic Services. After I had finished his story using notes he had typed up, he decided not to go ahead with the publication. But sadly, not long after that decision, Jim passed away. I felt that his story, like those of so many other air force, soldiers, sailors, and marines, needed to be told. Since Jim did not get a chance to edit what I had written, there may be some inaccuracies in what I am presenting, but it is still a remarkable tale.

A LONG WAY HOME

Chapter One

Henderson and I were running, or trying to run away from the inferno behind us. Fifty-caliber machine guns, their bullets set off by the ball of fire that had been the "Worrybird," were whizzing all around us. The fire turned night into day and ignited the ammunition and ordnance that we were supposed to have dropped to the French resistance fighters known as the Maquis. Like Fourth of July fireworks the explosives added a crescendo of noise to the roar of the fire.

On leg injuries sustained from the crash of our B-24 Liberator bomber, we hobbled down the hill, not daring to turn around to see what lay behind us. From the sound, we could tell there was nothing to see but a holocaust which had been our plane. With the help of the Maquis, we would spend the next three months evading the occupation forces of Germany.

The Maquis, pronounced ma'ki, were the predominantly rural guerrilla bands of the French Resistance. Initially they were comprised of men who had escaped into the mountains to avoid conscription into Vichy France's Service du travail obligatoire to provide forced labor for Germany. In an effort to escape capture and deportation to Germany, what had started as a loose group of individuals, they became increasingly organized. At first fighting only to remain free, with time, these bands became active resistance groups.

Originally the word Maquis referred to the kind of terrain, a type of high ground in southeastern France covered with scrub growth, in which the armed resistance groups hid. Members of those bands were called *maquisards*. Eventually the term became an honorific that meant "armed resistance fighter." The Maquis had come to symbolize the French Resistance.

Our job, under Colonel Wild Bill Donovan, head of the Office of Strategic Services, the OSS a precursor to the CIA, was to supply the

Maquis with supplies to fight a guerilla war against the Germans inside France. In addition to the American base at Harrington, England, the RAF was operating out of Tempsford. The missions were so secretive, that anyone leaking information about them would be treated as a traitor and could face severe punishment.

Our sortie started on April 27, 1944 in Harrington England. We were members of the 801st/492nd Bomber Group of the 8th Air Force. Our B-24 Liberator bomber was nicknamed the Worrybird after our mascot, a little wooden bird with a long beak and a sad face. We had a cage made for it in the sheet metal shop on the base, which we hung near the radio in the tail section of the B-24. As radio operator I was responsible for taking care of it. On this last mission, I had failed in my duties.

Before we could take off, the two pilots reviewed procedures, the gunners checked their weapons and equipment, and I busied myself with communications with the tower to eliminate any malfunctions before the flight. Activity was furious outside the plane where the ground crew was loading canisters with arms, ammunition, sabotage equipment, food, clothing, and other necessary aid for the resistance fighters. The canisters were to be dropped from about 600 feet, and unlike bombs, they would glide safely to the men waiting anxiously on the ground.

When I realized the Worrybird was not safely hanging from the hook near my radio, I went looking for him. I found him on the tarmac in a smashed cage, and like my heart, he was broken. He must have gotten trampled during the hectic activity around the plane and looking back, it could have been an omen of what was to come. Those of us who were not still busy loading supplies or preparing for the mission, did the best we could to straighten the mascot. Except for the worried look on his face, he was not the same.

Our mission, code name "Carpetbaggers," included twenty-one B-24's, including the Worrybird. Twenty would return.

The flight across the channel was uneventful and like all the other drops was at night. We were the second of two planes scheduled to drop near the same site. Ordinarily, flying at 600 feet near stall speed, we could see the people on the ground, but this time they were already at the first drop site about 500 meters, a third of a mile or 5 football fields from us. On our third descending circle from our flying altitude of 1000 feet, the Worrybird struck a hill.

Until the Baker Street London office of the OSS had recovered a French note, HQ assumed all aboard aircraft number 42-40997 had been lost. They were listed as: Lieutenant George W. Ambrose (pilot); Second Lieutenants, Robert H. Redhair (co-pilot), Arthur B. Pope (navigator), Peter Roccia (bombardier); Staff Sergeant Charles M. Wilson (engineer); Sergeants, George W. Henderson (tail gunner), James C. Mooney (dispatcher); and me, Tech Sergeant James J. Heddleson (radio operator).

The note from the French correctly listed three survivors but incorrectly reported that one of the survivors had been helped away from the aircraft by a woman who later turned him in to the Gestapo or he had been captured by them. The resistance people initially could not approach the wreckage because of the exploding ordnance. Attracted by the crash of the Worrybird, the reception committee was afraid that the Gestapo would confiscate the canisters dropped by the first plane. Therefore, they collected those supplies first and then sent some of the men back to the crash site where they found Sergeant Mooney.

The note went on to indicate that Ambrose, Redhair, Pope, and Wilson had been identified. There was an unidentifiable, badly mangled and burned body which was assumed to be Roccia. As bombardier, his station had been in the nose of the plane. In addition to the man who was later captured by the Gestapo, there were two others assumed to have survived and escaped.

A French historian later filled in what had happened on the ground. He stated that the earlier drop, which had occurred an hour previous to the Worrybird's arrival, drew the attention of the Germans. The second drop site target had been moved closer to the hills, no one realizing the hazard that change posed to the B-24. The target zone was a clearing surrounded by high hills and illuminated by reception lights. As the banking B-24 descended in circles, one of its wings struck a hillside causing it to career out of control.

What follows is my account of the mission, crash, and our eventual escape through occupied France.

As we arrived over the target area at two a.m., I received the signal "the umbrella is yellow." This radio signal was sent by the British Broadcasting Company to the resistance near St. Cyr de Valorges, in south central eastern France about halfway between Paris and Marseille. The message let us and the resistance know that the mission was cleared to proceed. With no more to do in the radio room, I proceeded to the camera hatch hole, directly behind Henderson's tail gunner position. He had removed the doors in case a quick exit was required.

Lt. Ambrose made a first pass for identification of the target and then circled around for the second pass and the drop. Wing flaps were deployed to slow the aircraft, the bomb-bay doors opened, and we started our descent. At five to six-hundred feet I could see men waiting for the sight of parachutes opening indicating that the canisters had been dropped. In addition to jettisoning the canisters from the bomb-bay doors, the doors had been taken off of the "Joe Hole" to allow Sgt. Mooney to toss out some other packages to the resistance. The Joe Hole was where the ball turret had been removed and doors installed. It was from the Joe Hole that secret agents parachuted using a static line on which to hook their parachutes.

After our descent to the lower altitude, the slow down, and the drop, we would immediately retract the wing flaps, increase speed, close the bomb-bay doors, gain altitude, and then return to the base at Harrington using evasive actions. Instead however, a wing hit something which I believed to be one of the hills surrounding the drop site.

The violent shaking of the plane threw me into an object where I struck my head just above my right eye. Another violent motion and I started to fall into the camera hatch, but my chest pack parachute stopped me. Noticing that I had been injured, Henderson, who had been strapped into his tail-gunner's position leaped out of the tail section and pulled me to safety. The bomb-bay doors started to close and the engines raced as if we had just completed our drop. Sgt. Mooney, who had been standing over the "Joe Hole," was gone. Because the plane was gyrating out of control, Henderson and I decided that it was best if we got out of the plane.

Before we could jump, we were thrown from the plane as it hit something again. The third hit and crash occurred moments later and the next thing that I was aware of was that I was lying on the ground, my parachute strung out in front of me. I did not recall that the chute had opened, it was just there on the ground and I was amid burning remnants of the Worrybird.

It seemed that I had hit the ground as soon as I had cleared the plane. My legs were hurting; I could feel some small pieces of metal in the back of my head and was sore in other places where bruises later would form. It was a miracle that I was still alive.

Shedding my Mae West Life Jacket and parachute, my attention was drawn to a large section of the plane. My training kicked in and before heading to the wreckage, I rolled my chute and hid it as best I could in the brush.

As I approached the piece of plane, I could make out in the dark and smoke filled atmosphere that it was a piece of the tail section. There was burning debris everywhere. I will never forget the intense heat from the roaring fire and stench of the spilled fuel which was feeding the fire.

Then Henderson came toward me from a direction opposite where I had been. We both must have been ejected when the section of the tail broke off. Our training must have caused us to pull our rip cords deploying our parachutes, and we must have been just high enough for them to get us safely to the ground. Our guardian angels were with us that day. We looked for Mooney but were becoming entangled in a mass of cables and wires. We called out for Mooney and the others as we started to distance ourselves from the wreckage. There were no responses. We found out later that all but Mooney had been killed in the crash.

Instead of his being rescued by a woman and turned over to the Gestapo as was initially reported, Mooney's back injury was such that the resistance could not take care of him, so they turned him over to the Germans for medical care.

A ball of fire lit up the night sky as we were heading for safety. Having no idea which way to go, we headed further down the hillside with the noise of exploding ordinance behind us. We assumed that everything that was supposed to be used in the resistance movement by the Maquis was now being consumed in the conflagration. Meant to protect the aircraft, the machine guns in the upper turret and tail sections – some of the very weapons that Henderson used against the enemy – were now firing in all directions.

Every step was agonizing on our inured legs, and not being able to see the terrain didn't help. We stumbled, limped, tripped, and fell our way about a mile and a half in random directions. Fear and shock kept us going until finally we stopped to rest. It was then that we decided to do everything we could to evade the enemy and not be caught only to spend the rest of the war in a prison camp.

Chapter Two

Prepared mentally to do all we could to evade the occupying forces, we checked our emergency kits. Because we feared that the use of matches would give away our position, we checked our compasses by the light of the moon. To the southwest toward the Pyrenees, was the mountain range which formed the border between France and Spain. That was the direction in which we headed.

In the distance was the glow of the fire lighting the area which would be crawling with the enemy soon. Those of us in the back of the plane had survived, while all in the forward section had perished. Although we didn't know for sure, we were certain that Mooney had survived too, having been in the tail section with us. Because the enemy would be looking for survivors, we did not rest too long. Later, there would be time enough for grieving for our fallen comrades, but now, in order to evade capture, we began our trek to the southwest.

The terrain was hilly and because we had kept to the woods, away from any traveled paths, our going was slow. At five-thirty in the morning, we stopped to rest our injured and tired legs. Our decision to keep to the woods had been a wise one. We later found out that the Germans had blocked off all the roads within a ten-mile radius of the crash site.

Our hastily hidden parachutes and other gear must have attracted the attention of the Germans. Soon after daylight, the roar of aircraft alerted us that the search was underway. German fighter planes, the Dornier Merkur 210 and bombers, the Junker 88, crisscrossed the sky skimming the tree tops searching for any surviving crew members. They were so close that the tree tops waved and twisted from the wake of the passing planes and we could smell the engine exhaust. I felt as though I could reach up and touch them.

Around eight a.m., the search slowed down. Climbing to the top of a hill only revealed the tops of houses rather than giving us much of an insight into the search activity. There was enough going on to convince us to wait. Hiding on the top of the hill, we waited until eleven-thirty before deciding to make our move.

"Does your head hurt?" Henderson asked.

"Yes," I responded. "Why did you ask?"

"Your forehead over your right eye is cut very deep and it looks bad," he said.

"What about the back of my head?" I asked, concerned about the shrapnel wounds.

"Hang in there and we'll take care of it the first chance we get."

His concern caused me to feel uneasy, but what else could I do?

Heading down the hill, we came upon a road. A quarter of a mile away, we could see a bridge that appeared to span a brook about seventy-five yards across. There was activity in that direction, but going away from the bridge appeared more risky.

"Let's head for the bridge", I proposed. "At least on the other side we can go down to the water and get a drink and wash up a bit."

"Sounds like our only option," Henderson agreed. "I'm thirsty anyway."

"Me too," I said. "We had best use our purifying pills too."

"Good idea," he said.

Just as we reached the other side of the road, our conversation was cut short by the sound of a truck coming toward us. Not taking any chances, we went down the hill and hid in the brush. The ravine and creek that were crossed by the bridge were just below us.

A truck full of grey-blue uniformed German soldiers roared by heading in the direction of the crash site. The swastika insignia on the truck confirmed the fact that we had just had our first close encounter with the enemy. We were frightened to say the least, and could not believe our luck at not having been spotted. As the truck headed away from us I could see a soldier in the back of the truck seeming to look right at us. As the truck moved further away and out of sight, he continued his stare obviously in deep thought about something. It seemed to me that the lower ranking German soldiers must not have been as well trained as their American counterparts. To this day I still wonder what was on his mind.

The creek below us was too wide to cross, so we decided to head for the bridge again. This time luck was on our side and we were able to get across the bridge and immediately into some nearby woods. Even though we had been traveling for hours, the way had been difficult and we had not gone very far from the plane. Avoiding any houses, people, or anything that moved, we traveled along the road for several more hours.

Realizing that we could not continue on our own any longer, we approached a house nestled in the woods away from the road. There we observed a man working on a small farm. By this time the air search had settled down to a plane or two.

"My leg is hurting really bad," I said.

"Stay put and I'll go and talk to the man," Henderson said.

With his hands extended and displaying in one hand his air force wings Henderson walked toward the man. Immediately, Henderson was taken to the man's house. He must have been aware of the downed aircraft nearby. After a short time, enough for Henderson to have explained our situation, the two of them came back to the woods and took me to the house.

The man spoke enough English and we enough French that we were able to gather that the man knew about the crash. In the house were the man's wife and two other men. They got across to us that they could help us, but it was too dangerous for us to remain. They fed us bread, cheese, and meat which tasted pretty good since we hadn't eaten since we had left Harrington, England. They also provided a basin of water for us to wash up, however; we could not wash anything more than our exposed skin as they remained in the room with us.

"There's a flap of skin on the back of my head," I said to Henderson as I washed my head. It was also tender to the touch.

"Don't move," Henderson said. "There are some pieces of metal in the wound.

He poured cognac on his knife and proceeded to dig out the pieces of metal. He then cut away some of the flap of skin.

"It's starting to smell bad," he said, and then poured cognac on the open wound.

Knowing that there was a twenty-five thousand franc ransom for turning over enemy flyers to the Gestapo, and that Henderson and I were not sure if these people were supportive or not, we decided to leave. There was a standing order for all civilians to turn in enemy flyers and the penalty for helping flyers, was to be shot on sight. They were probably anxious for us to leave too. One man had already left the house and we were afraid he was now turning us in.

Instead of returning with the Germans, the man came back with several hard-boiled eggs that his wife had made for us to take on our trip. The farmer took us back out to the woods where we had been hiding and told us to get some sleep. He said he would watch over us and we gladly complied.

After a short time, we were awakened by the farmer who handed us a pair of field glasses that he produced as if by magic. Pointing them in the direction of the distant hills, I looked through the glasses. From our vantage point, we could see at least a platoon of German soldiers loading up what was left of the Worrybird onto two trucks and driving away. Seeing that we had not come all that far was so disappointing that I almost cried, and we still had such a long way to go before we would be in Spain. The remains of the plane were barely recognizable. Where they were taking them, or what they were going to do with them we had no idea.

The presence of the Germans was obviously making the farmer extremely nervous. Taking some food from his pocket, he handed it to us, pointed in the direction we should go, and said "au revoir." We didn't hesitate any longer.

With hope in our hearts and thankful that we were still alive, we headed southwest in the direction of the French/Spanish border. On our cut and swollen legs we could not travel very far or fast on the hilly terrain. The rest of the afternoon, we walked about two-hundred yards at a time between rest stops. Around five o'clock, we stopped at a stream to fill our water bottles. We had only gone about a mile and a half all afternoon and were extremely exhausted. Keeping a watchful eye on an adjacent road, we lay down under some trees and rested.

An hour later, we started out again across an open field. About two hours later, after jumping a creek on our sore legs, we came upon another farmhouse and barn.

"This could be the home of one of the men waiting on the ground," I said to Henderson.

"Yeah," he replied. "But will our luck hold out? Don't forget that they get a reward for turning us in, and punished if they help us."

"You're right," I replied. "We'd better play it safe by hiding in the barn and head out early in the morning."

Suddenly, before we could reach the barn, our plan to not be noticed was spoiled as we were spotted by a small boy. Calling out to someone, he pointed in the direction of the house. Emerging from the house was a woman, who must have been his mother. As she approached us cautiously, we did the same.

Our concern that she might be afraid of us was alleviated somewhat when she pointed toward the barn.

Not until we were inside the barn did we relax, but guardedly so. When she arrived, we identified ourselves as Americans.

She knowingly shook her head and seemed to be aware that we had been on the crashed aircraft. Taking inventory of the barn, we noticed a large bed with no mattress, just bare springs. There was very little hay, but we saw no evidence of cows either.

"Should we stay or keep going?" I asked Henderson, as we both sat on the cot to rest our sore and tired legs.

"Traveling at night and resting by day doesn't seem to be a good idea now," he said. "Let's stay here tonight and then take off early."

That decided, we turned toward the woman, who in French, broken English, and some sign language got us to understand that she would be right back and that we shouldn't be afraid. When she left, we both fell into silence and awaited what would happen next.

Returning with food, watered down wine, and a blanket, she pointed to the bed and left. After eagerly eating and drinking, we covered the springs of the bed with hay and then spread the blanket over that. In our exhausted state, we both fell asleep immediately.

Chapter Three

Our plans to get an early start did not happen as we slept until eight o'clock. A shaking bed awakened us. Peering down to the foot of the bed we saw the woman milking a goat which she had tied to the bed. Seeing the bewildered look on our faces, she laughed, obviously amused at the way we had been aroused.

After she provided us breakfast and showed us which way to go, we thanked her. Apologizing for not being able to provide any further assistance, she gave us both a hug. We never saw a man nor did we ask where her husband was.

The direction in which she had pointed was the same one in which we had been headed, so we took off again toward the border. We traveled in silence for quite awhile until we came upon a set of railroad tracks.

"They look rusty and unused," Henderson said.

"Yeah, and they head south," I responded, after checking the compass.

"Let's walk it," Henderson said. "Nothing ventured, nothing gained, and it's easier than following the mountain terrain."

The tracks were set on a berm which led steeply down on each side. We could move to safety rather quickly, but the only way to go otherwise was along the tracks. After walking a while, we spotted a tunnel up ahead. Once in the tunnel, we rested our legs. They still bothered us, but we had stopped complaining about them. In addition to providing shelter and needed rest, the tunnel also hid us from German planes which were flying low over the countryside and might still be looking for us. After a short rest we headed toward the other end of the tunnel.

Emerging from the tunnel, we were in the center of a town, not unnoticed. Since we had been seen, running back into the tunnel would look suspicious, so we just continued following the tracks right through the town. With our gabardine flying suits and leather flight jackets, we were stared at and some people even waved, but nobody spoke to us. Waving back we continued on our way.

As we left the town, the houses got farther apart. An unfriendly looking old man was on the tracks walking toward us. Approaching him, we asked for help, but he became very jittery, waving his hands as if to shoo us away and shouted "partez, partez." We didn't need to speak French to figure out that he wanted us to leave him alone. The entire area must have known who we were and the trouble we could have brought to anyone associating themselves with us. We decided to be a lot more cautious from now on.

Because of our encounter with the old man, we left the railroad tracks and continued our escape through the woods. Before long, we came to a road which our compass indicated would take us south. It wasn't long before we spotted a truck heading toward us. It was about a mile away and since the woods were quite a distance away over flat, open terrain, we ducked into a nearby ditch.

As we lay as still as possible, the truck, full of German soldiers, roared past. We had not been noticed, but this second close encounter convinced us to stay off the open roads.

"We'd better stay in the woods even though it's hilly and the terrain is rough," I said.

"You're right," Henderson agreed. "My legs are still killing me, but the risk of getting captured is too great."

"My legs aren't any better, but you're right about the alternative," I said.

After a few miles in the woods, we came upon a small stream which afforded us the opportunity to get a drink and wash up a bit. The water tasted clean and sweet. Off in the distance was a small cemetery.

"Let's hole up in the cemetery for the rest of the day," I suggested. "Then we can resume our plan of traveling only at night."

Henderson nodded in agreement. It would be a short rest as it was mid afternoon.

Deciding to reconnoiter the area I walked around the perimeter of the cemetery. Down the road leading to the cemetery, I saw a farmer working in his garden.

"I saw a farmer down the road," I reported to Henderson when we approached each other.

"Let's ask him for some food," he said.

"My thoughts exactly," I said.

We must have startled the man as he jumped when we approached him. He was not prepared to see two "beat up" strangers in clothes dissimilar to the blue denim coat and pants that seemed popular in this region of France. He seemed reluctant to help us, so it was back to the cemetery and our original plan.

When we were only a few yards away, the farmer called to us in French. We looked back toward him and he was waving his arms. There were two of us and one of him, so we let him accompany us back to the cemetery. He must have changed his mind because he gestured toward a tomb and indicated that we should wait for him to return. If it was after dark when he returned, he would be able to find us if we stayed near the area he indicated.

Even though our first instinct was not to trust him, our being dirty and hungry made us change our minds.

"If he comes back with the Germans," Henderson said, "We'll split up and maybe one of us can make it out of here."

"Yeah," I agreed. "Instead of waiting out in the open, we can hide and see who he comes back with."

Our fears were ill-founded for within an hour, which seemed like an eternity, the farmer returned, smiling and carrying a note. When he handed it to me, I noticed that it was in English so I read it to Henderson.

"Teacher of school will come at five o'clock. Courage, we are your friends," I read, feeling relieved and happy for the first time since the crash.

Questions raced through our minds as we waited for the minutes to tick off until five. Is this the help we had hoped for? Are these men part of the Maquis? What would happen next?

Punctually at five, a man riding a bicycle and carrying a suitcase came toward us. He got off the bike and held open the suitcase for our inspection. It contained food, weapons, ammunition, and whiskey. I grabbed his hand and shook it to which he responded "savah." We took that to mean something like "okay." He seemed to be as happy as we were.

I was wondering how, or if we would need to use the guns when he produced some mercurochrome. He gently dabbed it into the wound over my right eye. The grimace on his face told me that he was concerned that I was in pain and that the wound did not look good.

The man started speaking to us in broken English for which he kept apologizing. We assured him that it sounded perfectly wonderful to us. He was the school teacher who had sent the note. Before riding away on his bike, he pulled the revolvers out of the suitcase and handed them to us.

"Use these if necessary," he said. "I will be back soon."

"Thank you," we said in unison.

At nine o'clock, he did return, on foot this time, with another man. This man was a walking arsenal, loaded to the hilt with weapons. Handing Henderson and I each a British made nine-millimeter, Sten submachine gun, he shouldered one himself and beckoned us to go with him. He and the teacher escorted us to the farmer's house. It was in the light of the farmhouse that I got a good look at the man. Like a Mexican bandito, his chest was crisscrossed with loaded bandoliers. In addition to the Sten machinegun, hand grenades were hanging from his belt which was also stuffed with two revolvers.

He's been watching too many John Wayne movies, I thought. *But he obviously means business.*

Bread, cheese, and wine were passed around and toasts ensued. The atmosphere was relaxed and not what we had expected. Finally, we were taken out and escorted to the schoolhouse on the other side of town. There was no hiding us as we paraded right through the center of the town. This sure was different from a few days ago when I was in my favorite pub near the base in Harrington.

More food and wine were consumed at the schoolhouse and I felt full for the first time since the crash. Feeling that we were among friends even under these dire conditions, I was not about to complain. Aware of who we were, the school teacher had told us that the Germans were looking for us using vicious police dogs. It must have been our crisscrossing of creeks and rough terrain that kept them from finding us before the Maquis. Because there was still a reward on our heads, Henderson and I remained guardedly relaxed.

Soon, the approach of a car could be heard. The garage door was opened and the car immediately entered. The door was shut before the driver and a female passenger could get out. Introductions were provided, but we believed the names were nick-names. I found out later that the schoolteacher's real name was Emile Benoit.

After more wine, in the dead of the night, the six of us piled into the car and we were taken to another farm. Relaxing in the car, I reached into the leg pocket of my flight coveralls and pulled out a Lucky Strike cigarette. My first puff brought an unusual reaction from all in the car except Henderson. They were all inhaling with me as the smoke from the cigarette wafted through the car. American tobacco was much esteemed in Europe, especially during the war.

"Would you like a cigarette?" I asked.

The car came to a halt and all of us enjoyed the tobacco.

"Here," I said, offering them the rest of the pack. "Keep it."

The cigarettes were divided politely among the four Maquis, while they thanked me profusely. Henderson and I felt safe in their care, but the thought of what would happen to them had we been stopped was bothersome. Henderson and I would probably have been beaten and taken to prison, but the resistance fighters would have been killed on the spot. The weapons we carried would have been of little use against the trained and seasoned German soldiers.

Turning around to speak to us from the front seat, with a reassuring smile the woman explained that they were not sure how to handle the situation since this was the first time they had harbored any Americans. She spoke fluent English and was able to answer all of our questions.

We arrived at another farmer's home where we had been told their resistance leader would meet with us. We were afforded the opportunity to bathe and shave for the first time in five days. The steaming bathtubs felt wonderful considering what we had been through. After cleaning up, we donned clothing that didn't fit. We both had to laugh when Henderson put on a woman's robe, complete with fur on the collar and cuffs. That night we slept between clean sheets, unafraid and grateful.

Chapter Four

On day six of our escape, we met a resistance leader who brought with him two women, an elderly man, and a doctor. It seemed as though all of France was filled with Maquis and that we had our pockets full of people willing to help. After putting liniment on our still swollen legs, the doctor took a look at my head wounds. My cheek was bruised, I had a black eye, and my wounds had started to heal. Grabbing a knife from his medicine bag, he poured alcohol over it and proceeded to re-open the cut over my eye. Even though he tried to be gentle, it hurt a lot. After pouring some more alcohol in the wound, he stitched it up with a plain needle and thread. He did nothing to the back of my head. I found out later that he was a veterinarian, but I considered myself fortunate to be afforded his services.

Conversation the rest of the day consisted of how we were to be returned to England. Our original plan of over the Pyrenees to Spain and then to Portugal, was discussed. Other methods were brought up such as: across the Alps into Switzerland where we would stay until the war was over, a boat to England from the coast of France, and even a submarine to Africa. Henderson and I just listened since we were not sure about our safety around our new companions and whether or not they were collaborators. We felt the less they knew about us the better off we would be.

After dark we were moved to an old abandoned building with nothing but four walls and a concrete floor. Since there was no furniture of any kind, we slept on the bare concrete floor. Once a day, a French man and woman brought us each a bowl of soup, a chunk of bread, and quart of water which was our provisions until the next day. The water was all we had for drinking and personal hygiene, which included shaving one day.

There was no toilet in the building, and of course, no toilet paper. A French newspaper was used for that purpose. To kill time, at first we tried reading the paper, but neither Henderson nor I could read French. So, when needed, we retreated to the farthest corner of the building and used it for its other intended purpose. As the French say, "c'est le guerre!"

We had noticed a good sized lake behind the building, but were told in no circumstances should we go to it. The chance of being seen, even at night, or perhaps betrayed by a barking dog was too great.

Alone most of the time, Henderson and I discussed taking off on our own again. Instead, we decided that this building with its obvious appearance of being abandoned, was a good hiding place until the others moved us someplace else. There we remained in total misery and discomfort for five long days while our fate was being considered.

At last, the resistance leader and the English-speaking woman came for us. We were pleased to be taken back to the woman's farm where we had been treated so well just five days before. She eloquently condemned the accommodations that we had been subjected to in the abandoned building. We were free to roam around outside her house and barn, both of which were enclosed by an eight-foot stone wall. Being her guest gave us a feeling of security and well-being. Best of all, we got another bath.

While we awaited our fate at the hands of the resistance, our gracious hostess taught us some French words and phrases. In return for her hospitality and to keep occupied, Henderson and I helped her hired hand (the only other occupant of the farm) with his chores.

"It is not necessary that you help around the farm," she told us, when she had noticed us helping. "It is enough that you are fighting for the freedom of France."

"Americans are also in this war," I countered. "We're fighting for our freedom too."

Our comfortable stay was not to last forever. A good friend of our hostess, a woman from the town, came to visit and couldn't help but notice us. Even though the visitor was a good friend of our protector, she was talkative. By noon the entire village was aware that American fliers were being sheltered at the farm.

The next day, the farm was invaded by German soldiers who came looking for us. Our luck was with us again as we were in the back part of the barn. As the Germans spread out in all directions, we were able to sneak out without being seen and hide in the nearby woods. From our vantage point on the creek bank, with forty-five caliber Colts drawn, we could see the soldiers prodding the hay in the barn with pitchforks. Had we been spotted, the small weapons we brandished would be no match for the arsenal the soldiers had with them.

At one point, three of the soldiers stood pointing towards the woods where we lay hidden, but to our surprise, they turned around and went back to the house. Our hostess's house was wrecked and she was bullied, but she insisted that there were no Americans there. She convinced them that the woman who had told the story about seeing us was actually demented. The Germans believed then that the woman had not been a reliable source and left without searching further. Had we been found, she would have been immediately executed. We lauded her bravery.

Early the next morning we were moved again to another farmhouse about six kilometers away. We met up with the chief of another organization who took responsibility for us. Our confidence had been shaken by the close call at the last house and we were again wary of our circumstances.

Our Maquis host this time was another leader, John Crozet, whom we found out, was known quite well by the Gestapo. His farmhouse was also surrounded by a stone wall with the barn attached to the house. From our room we could see the front gate. Warned one day to stay hidden in our room, we became curious as to what was going on. We looked out the window to see two cars entering the courtyard through the main gate. Getting out of one car was a Gestapo officer whom John greeted. They started talking and laughing as if they were old friends sharing a joke.

Several dozen eggs and a canister of milk were exchanged for an empty canister. We were told later that our host was the German's source of personal supplies that they didn't get from Germany. As the old saying goes, "keep your friends close and your enemies closer."

The next two weeks went quickly as we were kept busy around the farm acting like farmers. This made us more relaxed and kept our minds off our circumstances.

The twenty-fourth of May was the day Henderson and I got our French passports. An English speaking man took our information (name, rank, and serial number) and our photos, all of which was going to be sent back to Harrington to verify that we were who we said we were. The photos would also be used on fake passports. If we were not who we claimed to be, then we would suffer the consequences. We did not ask what those consequences would be since we had told him nothing but the truth.

The next night we were moved to St. Germain Laval and stayed for two days in a small apartment owned by another Maquis leader, Rene Simon. He was a serious man, but jovial, which gave our spirits a much needed lift.

Our next place of refuge was a house owned by a resistance leader, Jean Boyer. He was also a secret radio operator for this area of France. Daily, he would receive messages from England concerning parachute drops of arms, ammunition, and agents. If necessary he would also send a signal, but because the Germans were constantly looking for locations of transmitted signals, he did this rarely. The radio was hidden under the stair steps and, if found, would have meant a death sentence for Jean.

Quietly, at night, all types of guns (mostly Stens) were smuggled into Jean's house, which was more like the size of an American apartment with a fenced in back yard, than a house. But this was typical for many French towns. We kept our voices low so as not to draw the attention of Jean's neighbors. Henderson and I took on the task of disassembling the guns, which were covered with a rank smelling substance called cosmoline, and cleaning them. After reassembling the weapons, we stacked them until we had enough to take to the schoolhouse. At night, we would go to the school with the weapons and take them down into the basement for a test firing.

The school had been built around the thirteenth century and had four to five-foot thick walls. It was ideal for muffling the sound of the test firings. If any gun failed to fire, it would be taken back apart, fixed, reassembled and then test fired again. The finished, tested, and okayed weapons were then crated and taken to the various Maquis groups to be used against the detested Germans.

When there was nothing to do and boredom started to settle in, Madam Louise Boyer, Jean's wife, tried to teach Henderson and me some French words and phrases. It was as if we were having a French conversation class. We also played Bullit, a card game which pitted Henderson and me against Jean and Louise. During those card games, we spoke English and they spoke French. We enjoyed these card games laughing at times and eventually we would speak some French and they would speak English.

Even though food was scarce, they kept us fed with whatever was available, but no matter what they prepared, it was delicious. Once we were curious and asked what it was that we were eating. Jean pointed to some prepared meat and said "meow, meow." The expression on my face made him laugh very hard, but he assured me that it was just rabbit. Rabbits were raised by a lot of French families, so it was a staple at most meals.

On the next evening we got back the results of the report to London verifying our identity. London stated that they had been looking for us for over a month. We were also told that the rest of the crew members had been killed except Mooney who had been taken prisoner. Upon hearing this, Henderson and I sat down and cried for them. I vowed that they had died for a good cause and that they would never be forgotten.

One elderly man who used to accompany us on our evening strolls, M. Tournaire, we nicknamed "Papa Swing." His son, Joseph, had given up his bed at the Boyer house for us.

"Aller, Aller, Jimmy!" he would say when he came to the house after dark. "Promenade! Promenade!"

The nickname was created because of the way he came into the house snapping his fingers, acting as if he were dancing, and singing in broken English the song "Swing, Swing, Swing" from a Benny Goodman record. Donning sweaters or shirts and wearing berets in an effort to disguise ourselves, Henderson and I would take long silent walks around the little town of 800 with him, sometimes by the light of the silvery moon. If we recognized someone from the resistance, we would pretend that they were strangers lest we betray each other.

"Wake up! Wake Up!" Jean Boyer said at one o'clock one morning. "Come listen to the radio."

Henderson and I followed our beckoning host to the stairway where the clandestine radio was hidden.

"The invasion of France begins," an excited announcer was saying over and over.

It was June sixth, 1944, "D" day.

The message was clear urging the French resistance to step up its actions against the Germans. Transportation lines such as railroad tracks, bridges, and trestles were to be destroyed to impede the transport of German troops and supplies to the front. John Boyer was listening intently as people filled up the kitchen. Cognac and champagne appeared out of nowhere and a great celebration ensued. Buoyed up by the hopes that I would be home in a day or two, and as a result of the alcohol, I slept soundly the rest of the night.

Our early liberation and departure did not happen. It wasn't until the night of June nineteenth that we were told to get ready to leave immediately. We were taken to the home of Rene Simon who led us into a darkened room.

"Happy Birthday to Jimmy!" a group of people shouted, when the lights were turned on.

To my surprise, they had pooled their resources and produced a cake and ham sandwiches for my twenty-first birthday. I was now eligible to vote. I was told by the group that in the next election I was to "vote for no more wars!" I was deeply touched that these people, who were taking great risks for Henderson and me, cared enough to put together a party. Thoughts of my mother, who knew only that I was missing in action, came to me. If only she could see this.

The invasion did not stop our encounters with the German soldiers. A group of six very mean looking soldiers arrived in the town one day looking for two men. Not knowing if it was us or some other men whom they were searching for, we grabbed our Colt 45s and headed for the attic. We had made up our minds to put up a fight, if necessary. Looking out of the window, I could see the soldiers milling around with their weapons out and ready to use. Leaving by a back exit that led to an alley, we worked our way out of town ducking behind doorways as we went.

Through an open field, we made our way to a barn where we stayed until the patrol had left. When we returned to the town, we found out that the patrol had gone to the house of an old woman in search of her son. When she refused to tell them, in a Teutonic fury, they started to beat her until the son gave himself up to save his mother and left with his captors. No one had told the Germans about us, but we felt sorry for the poor woman and her son.

Emboldened by the invasion of France by the Americans, we joined the Maquis on some of their acts of sabotage. In broad daylight we raided different nearby villages taking what we needed from suspected collaborators. I remember one such episode in early July which I coined "The Great Tobacco Caper" led by Jean Boyer.

The plan was to "relieve" the village of their monthly ration of tobacco.

"If we succeed," Jean said, "the tobacco will be distributed to the Maquis who are hiding in the hills."

Because the village was too far to walk or bicycle to, we were to use a car. During the occupation, the Germans forbade the use of cars by private citizens, so we were not even supposed to drive. Also, the shortage of gasoline required that the car be converted to run on "gasogene."

Gasogene, or woodgas, is produced when wood, or charcoal, is burned in a starved oxygen environment. The incomplete combustion byproduct is a gas that can be burned in a combustion engine. The octane is much lower than gasoline, but the engine will run, although with a lot less power. A combustion chamber is provided in which a fire is started. As soon as enough fumes are created, the engine can be started.

There were five of us on Tobacco Caper, Henderson and I accompanied Jean and two other unnamed (for security reasons) Maquis. We had the Stens, which we had cleaned and reassembled, our Colts, and pockets full of ammo. We were all nervous and tense while discussing the raid and when Jean said something about "if we succeed," Henderson made a funny remark about succeeding. We erupted into side-splitting laughter, probably to disguise the fact that we were fearful. Another remark about borrowing a cigarette caused us to laugh even harder.

Ready at last for the mission, we left St. Germain Laval in the wood-fired car. Loaded with five men and supplies, the car did not have enough power to climb long grades. We pushed it on the hills, but on level roads, after a good stoking, it went pretty good.

At our destination, we ignored the looks from the townspeople, who probably suspected that we were the Maquis, but not that two Americans were with them. Henderson guarded the car leaving the doors open while I waited at the entrance to the tobacco store, keeping a lookout for anything suspicious. While the Frenchman went inside the store, I kept wondering if the car would be ready for a quick escape.

When they came out of the store, they were each carrying a burlap bag full of tobacco products. They motioned for me to collect several boxes from inside the store. When we had loaded all the tobacco in the car, there was not enough room for all of us to ride inside. Jean selected me to ride sitting on the outside of the car. I don't know the name, year, or make of the car, but it had those large headlights like the cars from the gangster age in the U.S. So, I sat on the right front fender with my legs wrapped around the headlight. My weapons were useless as I held on for dear life thinking that I was making a good target.

As we were making our escape from the town, a tire blew, but the driver did not slow down until it was safe to do so. I was jostled around until we finally stopped. Luckily there was a spare tire and while one man changed the tire, the rest of us stood guard.

"Maybe we ought to give up cigarettes," I said to Henderson, just to break the tension.

He broke out into laughter and then so did I. When we were able to relate in bad French to the others what I had said, and they were able to understand, they laughed too. I started to think that here we were, two Americans and three Maquis, with an outlawed car loaded with contraband tobacco, acting like children. Luck was with us again as we had been undetected by the Germans and had no more problems

When we arrived back in town with enough cigarettes to last us and the Maquis a long time, we celebrated our success as Chicago gangsters with some of our booty. When Henderson lit up a cigar, Jean referred to him as "Monsieur Capone." We were constantly aware of the danger we were in, but a sense of humor lifted our morale giving us hope and a positive outlook.

St. Germain Laval is located about fifty miles northwest of Lyon, what was, during the war, the second largest city in France. My hope of being back in England a few days after the invasion of France, was not to be. The Germans were still north of us and trying to get all of their supplies to St. Germain to fight the allied forces. The Maquis in this part of France were instructed to eliminate as many bridges as possible to impede the German's supply of men and material. Clandestine drops of arms and ammunition to the Maquis were keeping them supplied and the resistance movement was becoming more aggressive and involved in the war effort.

Chapter Five

On July eighteenth, Henderson and I were asked to participate in another Maquis mission with Jean and four other Frenchmen. We again were armed with the Stens, Colts, and ammunition, but instead of the wood burning car, we rode bicycles. Our destination was a railroad trestle, about twelve miles away, being used exclusively by the Germans to transport troops and equipment across the Loire River.

"This trestle definitely needs to be eliminated," Jean told us.

When we arrived at our destination, it was dark and very quiet. At the bottom of a valley, a long way down from us, we could see the river. At the river level, Henderson and I were told to be the lookouts while the Maquis attached the plastic explosives and the timing devices in strategic places around the bottom of the trestle. With this done, we retreated a short distance to watch the fun.

To the chagrin of the Frenchmen, the timers were not set soon enough as two German trains crossed before anything happened. A short time later, with a deafening roar, all hell broke loose as the timers functioned and the trestle was destroyed. With my ears ringing from the blast and adrenaline flowing, we rode our bikes up the hill and away from the area. Several times we ducked into ditches along the side of the road to hide from the enemy heading to what was left of the trestle.

Finally back at the house, my ears still ringing, I lay down and went to sleep thinking about what would have happened had a train been crossing when the explosives had gone off. The trestle being blown up by itself was a frightening thing to see as we had had to hide to keep from being hit by flying timber and other debris. Had a train been on the trestle, it would all have come crashing down upon us. The others considered this also and the possibility was the subject of conversation for many days after.

After a while, Henderson and I wore as our "uniform of the day" blue farmer's jackets and berets blending in with the populace and becoming Maquis ourselves. Since we had switched from being an American soldier to being part of the resistance and therefore spies, we no longer had the protection of the Geneva Convention. The fear of being caught either as a soldier or as a spy was always with us.

Our third mission with the Maquis came on July twenty-third. We were with the same men as the trestle bombing, and again rode bicycles. Instead of destroying any more infrastructure, we went to the home of a collaborator. Getting information and throwing the fear of God into them was our goal. When we arrived at our destination, we surrounded the house and our leader shouted directions to the people inside. Instead of coming out, their response to his demands was a perplexing throwing of furniture, chairs and tables, through the windows at us.

"We'll set fire to the barn unless you come out," our leader shouted.

This time they came out. Henderson took the women to one side to guard while the Maquis questioned the men. The questioning produced the desired results and the necessary information was obtained. As a token of their acquiescence, one of the women gave Henderson a large ham. It was a funny sight to see him riding the bike back to town with a ham dangling from the handlebars. The ham was a welcome change from the previous fare we had been living on.

The rest of our stay at Jean's kept us busy as we instructed the men how to disassemble, clean, and reassemble various makes of guns. We also taught them what we had learned in the gunnery school such as how to properly shoot a gun and how to lead and trail a moving target.

We in turn were taught basic French by Madam Boyer and soon we could understand and be understood speaking French.

On July twenty-seventh, four days after our last mission, the man who had sent the report about the crash of the Worrybird, visited us. All the information on us was confirmed and they now believed we were whom we said we were. Jean Pierre Etaix was my new name and I had a French passport to prove it. With a new set of clothes I was to be a farmer with a birth date of June 10, 1918, which made me a little older than my real birthday of June 19, 1923. So I wouldn't give my identity away by being asked questions, I was identified as a deaf mute. I hoped I could keep my mouth shut long enough to get out of France.

After giving us our new identities, we were told that we were going on a reception operation. Our job in the army had been to drop supplies to the Maquis. Now we were going to be on the receiving end of one of those missions working on the ground with those we had helped to win their freedom from the air. Just for luck, I donned my beret that night.

The trip to the drop site was in a car. In the back of the car was a "Eureka Set," which was a specialized radio worn on the back and used for communication with the pilot in the drop plane. Communication with the ground was crucial to finding the 400 to 600 foot radius drop zone. As soon as the engines could be heard, all worked as a team to make a successful drop right under the nose of the enemy. Since I was a radio operator I was given the job of signaling the plane with a flashlight, which would be returned from the plane. If the signals were all correct, the drop was on. I was used to being in the air using the moonlight to search the ground below. Now I was on the ground looking up for the airplane.

Unfortunately, there was no drop. Terribly disappointed, we all left in different directions for the night.

We received a message from the B.B.C. the next morning that "The astrologer fell in the well," meaning the operation was cancelled because it would have interfered with the parachute drops that the RAF was conducting. However, later that day, we received another message saying that the drop was on again for that night. Accordingly, we waited until it got dark and headed for the drop zone. While waiting for the drop, I had time to look around the area. To my surprise, in the distance was Jean Crozet's house where we had stayed for two weeks and where the Germans had gotten their supply of fresh eggs.

Soon we heard the distant noise of an approaching aircraft which made me tense with excitement and anxious to see what happened next. I didn't have long to wait as soon we had made contact with the pilot of the four engine RAF Sterling. On its first pass at about six hundred feet, I thought I felt the ground shake. I was able to signal the coded message and was rewarded with the "all correct" indicating everything was ready. The drop was on!

When the plane returned for the second pass, it was at about 2000 feet, which I thought was high for a drop. To illuminate the drop zone, the ground was lit with flashlights by the ground crew. Soon, twenty-four containers of arms and ammunition were on their way to us. With almost no wind, the containers stayed on track and did not drift away from the drop zone.

I wanted to talk to the plane, so I asked the Maquis leader to let me use the S-Phone (Eureka). Since this leader had not seen me before tonight's mission, he was reluctant and said "no." Rebuked, I joined the others in retrieving the canisters. Weighing about 300 pounds apiece, it took four of us to load them on four oxen-pulled carts. The oxen were big and slow, but they got the canisters to a waiting tractor where we transferred them from the carts to the tractor. Soon the canisters were in the Crozet barn, where we unloaded them and stored them away.

In the two weeks we had stayed at the farm, I had gotten to know the place pretty well. While at the farm, we were never told of, nor did we happen upon any stored resistance equipment, canisters, or any cache of weapons. That's how secretive these Maquis and the drop missions were.

When we were through storing away the canisters, we sat on the barn floor exhausted. One of us opened a canister and found the usual supply of arms, sabotage equipment, shoes, and canned food. Our host, Jean Crozet provided wine, and we opened some of the canned food and ate.

Before we left, Jean gave me a hug and in the French style, a kiss on each cheek.

"Moi American, oui?" he said. "I am so happy that you two Americans helped us tonight. It makes our countries that much closer than before."

The sun was coming up and with tears in my eyes, we said our goodbyes. On bicycles, cars, and on foot the team dispersed in different directions.

The next day, July nineteenth, 1944, Jean Boyer informed us that he had received word that we would be leaving his farm. We were to be taken back to England by air from a secret landing field behind enemy lines. It had been more than a year since we crash landed and the next morning, we would begin our journey back to where we had started.

We gave up our uniforms, including my leather flight jacket, for civilian clothes. So there we were with our fake passports, dressed in suits with ties and of course a beret, saying our goodbyes. Feeling like a Frenchman, I was still aware that if we were caught we would be shot as spies. It was a bittersweet occasion as we said our goodbyes to our comrades in arms. We were sad to go, but they and we were happy that finally we would be going home. Our trust was now in those who were in charge of seeing us to our rendezvous with the aircraft.

The small truck that we were riding in only stopped once and that was beside the crosses marking the graves of our fellow crewmen who had died in the crash. Saddened by this emotional goodbye, we said a prayer over their markers and we vowed that we would never forget them.

About three kilometers farther down the road, we passed the scene of the crash of the Worrybird. Bits and pieces of the plane lay about the scarred and burnt ground. A shudder went through me as I wondered how Henderson and I had been able to survive that night.

Our destination was finally reached and we spent a comfortable night in a small hotel.

As we sat on the terrace of the hotel, sipping some drinks, a group of German soldiers rode past us on bicycles. They all had the Sten machine guns which had probably been taken from the Maquis. When they slowed down and stared at us I was frightened inside, but I stared back showing no emotion. Thinking that we had come too far for this to be the end, we decided that surrender was out of the question. But, to the relief of everyone on the terrace, they kept going without stopping. My guardian angel must still have been with me.

The message signal for the clandestine operation to airlift us out of France was "Moon of July." That day, the message was received at 1330 hours and again at 1930 hours. However, at 2130 a cancellation message was received, so for security reasons we were moved from the hotel to a farmhouse on the outskirts of town.

In addition to the farmer's rather large family, there were Henderson and I and five other escapees. They consisted of three spies, a Canadian

Spitfire pilot, and a British Lancaster navigator. The table groaned under the banquet of food for nineteen people.

The next day we were separated and Henderson and I were relocated, yet again, to another location. By car we were taken to a Maquis liberated town where the townspeople were almost all armed with firearms, even the women. We felt safe enough to be able to walk freely around the town, where most people, knowing that we were Americans, wanted to shake our hands.

A woman about my age, brandishing a Sten machine gun and a loaded bandolier over her shoulder, approached me.

"Would you write to me after the war?" she asked, obviously aware that I was an American, even without a uniform.

"Of course," I said.

She wrote her address on a piece of paper and gave it to me. Later, realizing that she would not be safe if I had been caught by the Germans and they found her address on me, I tore it up. I wondered if she remembered me and what would have happened had I written to her. As the French say, "C'est la vie."

That day, a car arrived and took us back to the hotel where we had been staying. I wondered about our other escapees, but had a feeling that we would be seeing them again soon.

Another day and another canceled flight. Since so many variables were at play, the escape flight was subject to a lot of changes. Foremost was the necessity for a full moon to light the landing area. It was waning and we dreaded another month's stay behind enemy lines.

For the next two weeks, we were entertained by a new Maquis protector, Charles Beraudier. Using a French-English dictionary to communicate, he told us sad stories about all the friends he had lost to the Germans. The rest of the time was spent swimming in the Soane River, basking in the sun, and sharing wine. The fun times and laughter we shared made us feel as brothers and I will never forget him.

Finally, on August tenth, we were told that the flight was definitely on. The flight was cleared all the way to England and we were escorted by carloads of armed Maquis to a small village named Manziot, approximately ten kilometers away. Nearby, in an open field with no runway, we were greeted by a Maquis chief, Paul Reviere. He was in charge of all landings in this area and had recently been to Harrington, where he had spoken to my commanding officer, Col Heflin. It was during that meeting that he had arranged for Henderson and me to return. Also at the field were the other airmen and spies whom we had met before. It was a wonderful feeling of camaraderie as we greeted each other with handshakes and hugs.

Because there was a large group of German soldiers stationed nearby, the field was surrounded by about 400 armed Maquis. If the Germans had any idea what was going on, in light of the large force of resistance fighters, they were showing understandable reluctance to do anything about it. At 0130 hours, the field became active.

The perimeter of the field was illuminated with flashing lights from handheld flashlights just as we heard a plane. As it circled, I noticed four lights in the shape of the letter "L" in the middle of the field. This was a signal to the pilot indicating in which direction to land. I recognized the plane as a Lockheed Hudson and with its landing lights on, I thought it was the most beautiful sight in the world.

After the plane landed and turned around, we had a scant six minutes to line up and get on board. There were seven of us with number three and four priorities, giving us precedence over lower numbers. As soon as we were on board, the plane started to rev the engines for takeoff, even as the doors were still being closed. It was the most wonderful feeling, after five months behind enemy lines, that in five hours I would be back at the base in England.

Those left behind: the brave Maquis, whom I had come to know as brothers; my lost comrades beneath five white crosses in a small cemetery in France; and Sgt. James Mooney, somewhere in a prison hospital, were deeply in my thoughts during that five-hour flight. The flight was uneventful, no spotlights, no flack, nothing to impede us. It certainly had been a long way home.

PART FIVE

Poetic Stuff

From a Christmas Card:

This holiday season I wish you pleasure, but something else that you
must treasure.
Joy and happiness last for eternity, while pleasure is only temporary.
So search your heart and keep in mind, those near to you is where
you'll find
joy to last when we are gone, and happiness when there is no dawn.
Giovanni

I wish that my parents could have been here to see the fruits of my labor from my first two books, *Dedra* and *Moonbeam*. Mom and Dad are in a higher place, and I know that they are watching as they did when I was growing up. I caused them a lot of grief in my childhood as you can ascertain from the stories in *Moonbeam*. I was lucky enough to have them as parents. My three sisters and I had few material possessions growing up, but my parents made up for it in other ways. They left me more than enough resources enabling me to get my first books published. The talent to write was inherited and the skills were developed under their encouragement.

The first two poems to follow were written after my mother's death. For the last several years of her life she suffered from the incredibly cruel disease of Alzheimer's. She took a copy of the first poem with her when she was interred. You may notice the word Mom vertically repeated with the first letter of each line, hence the title "Symmetry."

Symmetry

MOM,
My life began
Only you felt the pain
More than the pain you felt
Of a son being born
More likely it was love
Of giving life to me
More than that I cannot feel
Only now you feel no pain
Mostly because your life has ended.

MOM,
My pain you felt
Only You
Many times
Only you were there
My tears would fall
Only you would dry up the
Moistened cheeks of my youth.

MOM,
Many years have passed
Of that there is no doubt.
My only wish was that I could have
Only absorbed the pain you felt.
Much to my dismay I cannot take away any
Of what you may have felt in the past years.
Misty are my eyes now.

MOM,
Maybe I realize now
Only you could have given me life.
Maybe now you are at peace.
Oh yes,
Maybe we will be together again.
On that I could
Mostly
Only hope.
My love to you,
MOM.

Mom's favorite flower was the rose and upon her casket a bouquet was placed before burial. One of those flowers was given to me and when it had dried I wrote the following. The rose still rests in an honored place in my house.

A Flower Is Gone

A seed is planted.
It swells and pushes through the earth
the sun shines brightly
a beautiful flower is given birth.
Above the weeds
the flower struggles to reach a height
to be washed
in the morning light.
From the sun and rain and earth
the beautiful flower will be nourished,
and near the end of spring
the beautiful flower will have flourished.
Its beauty and radiance
glow throughout the summer
giving joy and pleasure
causing all who pass by, awe and wonder.
When fall begins,
the flower sends its seeds to earth
for generations of new flowers
in each spring will be given birth.
And in the fall
the beautiful flower's life begins to wane
its life's work is done
it will not be seen again.
But those who saw
the flower in the light of dawn
will always remember and regret,
Now that the beautiful flower is gone.

When it was my father's turn to join her three years later, I wrote a poem for him and read it at his showing. He suffered indirectly from the effects of her Alzheimer's. During the last three years of her life in a nursing home he visited her every day, ensuring that she would at least eat one good meal. I witnessed his love for her as never before and then his heartbreak when she was gone. His broken heart eventually took him. His poem deserves this explanation:

Until three of us left the nest during the same year, Dad always had had at least two jobs. He worked hard just to keep food on the table, a roof over our heads, and clothes on our backs. For most of the seventeen years that I lived with them, he had the same job with a monument company. He was a terrific artist, designing and sandblasting drawings on monuments in the shop. The sand from that work, eventually affected his lungs such that he had to use oxygen during his last two years.

The monuments were usually sold when someone had died. Along with the names and any other information, the full date for the person who had died was sandblasted in the shop. If there were two people to be buried side by side, the death date for the second person was left blank. When the second person was interred, the death date had to be completed in the cemetery. Dad, as one of his second jobs, did that.

To get a portable compressor and sandblasting equipment necessary to cut the stones in the cemetery, Dad, his helper and friend, Harry, and I drove to Buffalo, New York in our brand new, blue and white, 1954 Dodge station wagon. That vehicle had been bought specifically for carrying the portable sandblasting equipment. On that trip, we ate and slept in the car.

On the good-weather weekends, as soon as I was old enough to help, Dad and I traveled to the various cemeteries within two-hundred miles of our home in northeast Ohio.

After we found the cemetery, we looked for the specific marker in need of the added numbers. Most of the time, freshly-heaped dirt on the recently dug grave marked the location. At other times we had to hunt. My main job was to help him offload the large portable compressor, sandblasting tank, hoses, and other tools.

If he had more than one stone to finish in the same cemetery, I looked for the other markers while he set up. Otherwise, I would bury my head in a book. The first few times that I went with him, everything was new to me and I just watched him work. With the equipment in place, he would carefully lay out a self-sticking rubber pad where the numbers went, and trace the letters from a stencil. Then with a sharp X-acto knife, the numbers were carefully cut out leaving bare stone where the sand could notch the letters into the granite. My most important job was to verify that we had the correct marker and that the date he was preparing to cut was correct according to the work order. A mistake could cost him a year's pay.

The entire process took about thirty minutes per stone. For this he received a portion of the $15 his company would collect. The poem, *Stonecutters Lament*, recalls the process, and raises an unanswered question that I'm sure Dad thought about each time that he cut the last two numbers.

Stonecutter's Lament

A soul is gone and placed in the ground
a stone marks where he was laid down.
Four lonely numbers on a line forlorn
announce to all when he was born.
Two other blanks on the line await
someone to finish the ending date.

A stonecutter searches, the stone is found.
He lays his tools upon the cold ground
and kneeling sheds a tear, as if in prayer.
Before the stone he does prepare
where it is blank to add two numbers deep
a reminder forever this date to keep.

And when the stonecutter's job is through,
he checks his work to make sure it's true,
and deep within he wonders when it's his time,
whose tears will cut the stonecutter's final line?

This poem was inspired by someone whom I fell in love with, long ago.

An angel from the past.
Her touch was gentle and warm.
Her kiss was as sweet and moist
as the morning dew.
Her closeness filled me with joy.
Her fingers on my face and the touch of her lips
sent wisps of fog through my mind.
She took me to her cloud.
She held me there floating
with the gentle wind that surrounded us.
She melted my soul into darkness. Then,
she lit the night with her glow
like the moon on a clear October night.
An angel from the past.
I know what it's like;
what it's like to float,
to float on a cloud,
on a cloud with an angel,
with an angel in my arms.
In my arms and in sweet embrace,
in sweet embrace holding on,
holding on with gentle kisses.
Gentle kisses and warm feelings,
warm feelings and stirrings,
stirrings deep inside.

We float above all else,
all else below forgotten.
Forgotten pains forgotten hurts,
hurts of long ago she makes them all,
all seem so far away and now,
now I have new visions.
Visions of the future,
a future full of joy.

Joy and love and then,
then she carries me,
carries me back to earth.

And as we part it is;
it is as if I am held,
held to earth, but now I know;
know that I can float;
float on a cloud,
on a cloud again with an angel,
with an angel in my arms.

A lost love inspired another poem while I was picking elderberries at the apartment I lived in shortly after my divorce.

Elderberry Pickin'

Will you go elderberry pickin' with me?
They grow almost anywhere, you see.
Out in the woods, or down by the sea.
By the side of the road near an old oak tree.
In an open field wild and free.

We'll trek hand in hand, at each other we'll smile.
We'll walk a few feet, or maybe a mile,
and if we get tired after awhile,
we'll sit on the grass the time to wile,
counting ants in the grass marching single file.

Eventually we'll find the treasure we seek.
The little bright berries so ripe at their peak.
The clusters from the bush put into our basket to keep,
and then when I know you're not looking at me,
I'll admire your beauty with a quick peek.

When we have a full basket and begin to tire,
and the sun is too hot making us feel we're on fire,
we'll stop the pickin' and to the backyard retire,
to clean the berries attached to the stems like a wire,
and soon the pile of berries grows higher and higher.

And our basket of berries shrinks to a few,
we laugh at the color of fingers so blue,
and steal a kiss one for me one for you.
Elderberry pickin's not about the gathered fruit,
it's about the time alone together, just us two.

So tomorrow, the next day, and as far as I can see,
will you go elderberry pickin' with me?

Inspired by another lost love.

Could I have been the stream
flowing around the swells of your breasts,
licking at your soft skin,
caressing your nipples as I cooled you off,
wrapping around you, front to back,
holding you gently in an embrace until
you were satisfied?
If I only could...

These two poems were a result of the forlornness after my divorce. The first was written shortly after I had moved back to my home town and, while jogging, I noticed that the sidewalks where I had grown up were now deteriorating as my marriage had done.

The second poem was when I noticed in a park, two trees on either side of a road where one tree appeared to reach across to touch the other. The poem is written in a visual as if it were the one tree that was reaching across the road toward the other.

Crumpled Sidewalks, Broken Dreams

When the sidewalk was laid down
it was to serve a brand-new town.
Those with a hope, a plan, a dream, a goal
tread o'er the slate, sandstone, and marble.

Two lovers hand in hand strolling in the nights,
chalk marks for hopscotch and kids on bikes,
the sole postman delivering mail,
all used the sidewalks to their avail.

Saplings were planted close by the side.
Into trees they grew, shade they did provide.
But the years passed by and soon transformed,
the level sidewalks were soon deformed.

The roots of the trees upheaved the stone,
the children who played there all have grown,
the lonely postman does not walk by,
and lovers don't stroll side by side.

Just like our dreams that once were level,
but through the course of time become disheveled,
deterioration from wear taking its tolls,
and the realities of life uproot our goals.

Unless we mend the sidewalks of life
as they wear down or break from strife,
correcting the course where the path is craggy
so we won't stumble on our life's journey.

Or else our journey will have been in vain.

Two Trees

The tree I saw this morning formed an umbrella across the road.
It was reaching for the other side, another tree to hold.
Both the trees were young once, they grew so fast and full.
The one which stretched across the road finally reached its goal.
But, in taking so long to span the rift, the other had grown cold.

    A rejection of the stretching one,
    to leave it frail and old.
    It was as if a love
    that flourished
    to span between
    two souls, and
    once they had
    finally touched
    the other had
    new goals. With
    life almost at end
    It left the growing
    one dismayed
    to stand a short
    while longer
    with roots and
    life decayed.

While living in Vermont, I was a volunteer driver for the Red Cross using their cars to transport people to doctors and medical facilities. The roads in rural Vermont traverse many wooded and unpopulated areas teeming with wildlife. I wrote this little fun piece and gave it to the dispatchers who always gave me my assignments. They enjoyed it, or so they said.

The Borrowed Car

I'm returning your car, but in the trunk in the rear
are a fender, an angry dog, and a bear's ear.
If you'll give me a minute I'll tell you the story.
It's not what you think and it's not all that gory.

I was driving a little fast down a quiet country road,
when out of the woods jumped a bear chasing a toad.
I slammed on the brakes trying to avoid a collision,
but the wet slippery pavement gave the tires no adhesion.

So what occurred next you're likely to guess
was the bear and the fender making a mess.
Thump, thump was the sound that I heard just then
as I ran over the bear, again and again.

I backed up to retrieve the fender, which came off in the ruin.
Thump again went the rear tire as I rolled over the bruin.
I stepped from the car and saw an interesting sight.
The bear's head was sticking out from under the car on the right.

To save me again from hitting the creature,
I bent and grabbed hold of the bear's prominent features,
which was, as you guessed the only parts I could grip,
the ear in my left hand and in my right its upper lip.

I tugged and I tugged and I dragged the large beast
out from under the car and away from the street.
I thought one more tug and the bear would be clear,
so I gave a heave ho which pulled off his right ear.

A lucky day for the bear as he was okay.
He jumped up from the spot where he lay,
and shaking his head he scampered away,
but it wasn't going to be my lucky day.

After the bear's escape I looked up to behold,
the car on its own had started to roll.
It seems that in neutral was how it was left,
and the emergency brake I never had set.

So picking up the fallen fender I started to race
after the car down a hill and off the road I gave chase,
through someone's yard which had, to my remorse,
a doghouse in the front yard inhabited of course.

Straight through the doghouse the car did lumber,
hitting the dog inside while he was at slumber.
The car headed toward a house where sat an old woman
up on a porch in a chair. She never saw what was comin'.

As I was wondering what else could add to my woe,
the car jumped up on the porch knocking her through a window.
The trunk in the rear popped open in protest,
as the car flew off the porch and came to a rest.

So I tossed in the front fender and looking down
the ear of the bear still in my hand I had found.
So I tossed that in too and for a good measure,
I heaved in the stunned dog to add to my treasure.

The woman was cursing as loud as she could,
so I knew she was all right, but not in a good mood.
I slammed the trunk shut and hiding my face
hopped into the car to get out of that place.

I started it up and tried to put it in gear
trying first, second, and third, soon it was quite clear,
that reverse was the only transmission mode.
So I backtracked through the yard and onto the road.

Past the spot where this all started, I was backing.
I noticed that toad by the road, he was laughing.
So I reversed your car all the way back to you
going as quick as I could passing only a few.

When I got back to your place I was quite relieved.
The dog had revived but biting mad as can be.
He's snarling a lot and growling don't you see,
if I opened the trunk he would surely attack me.

So everything that I thought could identify you,
I brought back, as much as I could, and I'm telling you true.
Your car is a mess and the transmission is scorched.
Oh, by the way, your license plate fell off on the porch.

After reading one of those women's magazines with the silly questionnaires, one of which said to ask your husband what he thinks your best features are, my wife, now ex, asked me. Without hesitation and to be funny, I replied, "your elbows," which became a running joke for many years. It was one of those never-let-me-forget answers, so I tried to make it up to her with this poem.

Features

If asked about your features,
I would have to say:
The smoothness of your skin,
the way it tastes today.

The softness of your lips,
and the sparkle in your eyes.
The scent in the bend of your neck,
the warmness of your thighs.

The darkness of your hair,
in the candlelight it glows.
The dimples in your cheeks,
whenever your smile grows.

Your breasts so sweet and nipples firm,
the tip of your nose I love to kiss.
Your ears so sensitive to my breath,
your supple fingers tips.

I wouldn't want to single out,
and say one feature is your best.
To ignore one or the other,
would belittle all the rest.

Your physical features are,
just a place to start.
There are things I cannot see,
like the love dwelling in your heart.

You do have other features,
too numerous to count.
You are intelligent and determined,
to do all the things you want.

As with everyone of us,
you go through times of stress.
But I love you through the worst of times,
waiting for the best.

You are the standard I would adopt,
if ever I needed to.
Should I even live forever
I could never replace you.
Love, your adoring husband and partner through life.

A poem inspired by an ice storm one March morning.

Tuesday, March fourth, freezing rain hit our town.
I cursed the storm that brought it around.
A glassy mess was coating the street,
my car, my house, and even my feet.

I was tired of winter. With this latest blast
it came in unwelcome and threatened to last.
Entering the house, both shivering and wet,
I closed the door then to bed, disgusted, I went.

I grabbed a book from the shelf on the right,
prepared to read, maybe all through the night,
but soon was tired and fell asleep really late,
lulled by the pitter-pat from the roof made of slate.

I don't sleep past the rising sun I can boast,
but twas dawn's light when I stirred and then I arose.
I crossed the room very slowly, eyes filled with sleep,
to the window I went lifting the shades for a peek.

My eyes opened wide, my mouth followed suit,
when results of the storm's wrath came into view.
For every bare tree, bush, and twig on the ground
was bent and coated with ice all around.

It was as if God had left a message for us.
Into liquid diamonds he dipped his brush.
Painting a scene for our eyes to take in.
A reminder that all was created by Him.

For our ears too, he played a soft song.
Gentle winds persuaded that the trees go along.
They moved just a little sending a creak and a moan
that added to the glistening with a varying tone.

Winter is forgotten with the change of the season.
That storm was for us, it was sent with good reason.
A reminder from our Maker to us all, that we should,
accept that which was bad, remember that which was good.

I was honored to have a robin build a nest in a planter on the balcony of my second-story apartment. When the babies had grown and taken flight, I sadly noticed an abandoned egg still in the nest.

The bird on my porch wove a nest of grass
taken from a field grown the summer last.
She placed four eggs the last fortnight morn.
Three have hatched, but one unborn.

The egg sits there 'neath the ones who live.
No one to love no one to give
care and warmth an embryo furled
inside a shell all withered and curled.

The others get strong and soon take flight,
and leave their crib on the morning light.
The one remained I carefully take
to a shelf in my den a place that I make.

I am not able to give it life,
but there is a joy it does provide.
To a child's eyes which open wide
to view the gem and ask, what's inside?

Another silly love poem to an unrequited love.

The lonely sailor walks down to the sea,
He hears the voice of his love far away.
Like the Greek Sea Nymph, Siren,
she calls him, her words an echo
bouncing at him from all directions.

His heart aches in his chest for her.
His thoughts of her cloud his mind.
As he is about to lose his resolve,
the echo returns, luring him to the water's edge.
A dolphin jumps near shore, beckoning him.

He feels his soul melting. Melting into the sea,
becoming one with the water, and drawn outward.
Like the ray, he glides through the depths,
his essence, like the ray's wings, take him ever closer to her,
until he can feel her presence all about him.

He feels her enveloping him, holding him, caressing him.
They are as one in the depths, together in thought,
together in love, together in each other.
Sadly, he must return to his place, and she to hers.
Slowly he goes yearning for the time when their union is of the
    flesh.

While my wife, now ex, and I lived in Japan, we traveled to Hong Kong at least three times. On one of those trips, we purchased a diamond for my wedding ring, one which we could not afford when we had gotten married. In fact, her first ring was plastic and made a funny plunk sound when placed on the gold plate for blessing by the priest. We later got her a real gold ring and then a diamond ring. I never had a wedding ring until we purchased the diamond in Hong Kong and had it mounted in Okinawa, where we lived for five years.

After thirty years of marriage, I took the diamond from the ring, had it made into a pendant, and gave it to her as a thirtieth anniversary gift. When she divorced me a couple of years later, she kept the pendant.

This Diamond

This diamond took thirty thousand years
to grow into a glowing gem.
My love has grown for thirty years
to a glowing fire within.

It may have taken another thirty thousand
to find it in this place.
My heart has in thirty found
a true love I can't replace.

This diamond will last thirty thousand more
and always be a treasure.
My love will last forever more
and grow too large to measure.

Close to your heart let this gem be
and always keep it true
Remembering that it means to me
my undying love for you.

The following series of "love poems" were inspired by various women while searching for love after my divorce.

Two clouds form in the desert sky,
heart shaped puffs of mist.
They are the dreams of you and I,
two shapes of willowy wisp.

The heat from the sun the sand below does bake
raising currents from the desert floor.
Urging the hearts together one shape to make,
a single heart forevermore.

And as the day turns into starry night,
the reddened shapes seem to evanesce.
From those below gone out of sight,
but not from the two of us.

Shooting Stars

Two ancient lovers meet on a mesa
'neath the stars on a moonless night.
Their faces show the passing of time,
but their spirits are young and immortal.

As their bodies join together,
two falling stars streak across the sky,
burning together brightly for a moment
marking the heavens as they have each others' lives.

Super Nova

We are like two distant stars
in different galaxies
which may never meet.
For if we did,
we would join and
collapse within one another
consuming everything
that is near, even ourselves.

Left at a distance
we will continue to brighten
just our portion of the universe
for a longer time.
But then, the heavens
will never know
just how spectacular
we could be as one.

Only time will determine
if there is a force
which could draw us
to each other, closer,
to a point of no return
where there is nothing
that could keep us apart.
We may never know.

Floating

We float together in the air
like two leaves in a breeze
twisting togther spiraling
in the twisting currents.

Our connection is love
joining us in a dance
a pirouette of life.
We move as one but separate.

Together yet apart,
where we are drifting
we do not know,
but we are going together.

Untitled

Your voice was like listening to the wind whispering in the trees and the soft fall of water along a brook. You lift me higher each time we speak.

We are as two heavenly bodies pulling each other inward. Accelerating nearer and then missing. Giving each other energy to spin back out into another orbit. An orbit that will bring us closer next time. Will the pull we exert on each other cause another near miss, or will we join as one, lighting the heavens, brighter than anything the universe has ever conceived?

A Diamond

Like a diamond in a sea of sand,
a gem like no other, alone you stand.
I was looking, searching for something, someone,
when a chance glint of light beckoned me come.

A ray of light held out toward me
from one so bright upon the sea.
I followed the glow until I found, knowing
here was a soul so warm and glowing.

Ten-thousand karats could not compare
to this diamond I found, you are so rare.
To touch the diamond's perfect cut and feel you,
to bring it to my lips and taste you,
to gaze deep through a surface strong yet thin,
to see perfect color and clarity deep within.

I hold the diamond to my heart
and pray that we will never part.
I abandon the search o'er the sea for another
This gem I strive to keep nigh forever.

Until

The wine was cool
her lips were warm.
I, giddy as a fool
enwrapped by her charm.

We lay side by side
in embrace so tight.
The hours did fly
day changed to night.

I can still taste
her lips so sweet.
Time make haste
until again we meet.

Untitled

The mid morn I await, for an angel to date,
one so delicate it makes the rose petal weep.
Within me nerves jingle making my hands tingle.
My crown is a swoon, my legs feel very weak.

Soaring

Teach me to fly, teach me to soar.
Take me with you forever more.
Together we'll be above the world
our inhibitions all unfurled.

Like birds on high catching the winds
the warm air rising lifting our wings.
We'll join together and make sweet love.
Our troubles below us, we sail above.

We return to earth when we are sated
with spirits high and souls elated.
Our soaring over for a short while,
we gaze at each other with a knowing smile.

While on the earth we keep our eyes
elevated toward the heavenly skies.
When we are done with our worldly chores,
again we'll fly, again we'll soar.

The Mermaid

To the beautiful mermaid in the depths of the sea.
Someday in the future I hope you meet me.
We'll join together and live eternal life,
free from harm and everyday strife,
and make love on the mountain and on the beach in the sand;
twice if by sea, once if by land.
It's too bad mermaids have no feet below.
I'd really like to nibble a toe.
You have no fun parts below the waist.
I'll have to settle for sashimi to suit my taste.
When you read this poem you'll think I'm a nut;
however, when you swim away I'll say "what a butt!"

I Want To

bring joy to your life, never make you sad;
make you laugh, never cry from pain;
keep you warm inside, never leave you cold;
be with you always, never leave your heart;
become one with you, never be apart.

Your Feel

The lightning flashed shadows across the wall,
while the thunder echoed through the windows.
I reached out to snuggle and wrap my arms around you,
but you were not there.
I imagined what it would be like joined to you.
Your back cuddled against my chest, your legs bent around mine,
my arms about you pulling you closer feeling your warmth.
So close we were as one, breathing in unison.
Our hearts in rhythm like the sound of raindrops against the
     window.
I drifted off to sleep as the storm subsided,
while the thoughts and feel of you stayed within me.

Who Was It?

It started with a gentle wind, and then...
Rain. It pattered on the roof. Little drops at
first, but then it beat ferociously against the
bedroom windows. Laying my book aside
I decided to call it a night and let the drum beat
of the rain lull me to sleep, but...
Halfway to unconsciousness and the relief it brought
me these lonely days, I heard a rustling noise
intermingling with the rhythm of the storm.
"Who's there?" I called out. No answer. I shut my
eyes, hoping it was a dream. When I opened them a
fraction of a second later, there she was. Standing at
the foot of the bed was a woman. Or was it? It was an
image, rippling in the dim light streaming in from the
light of passing cars. It was as if I was looking at
her through rain washing down a window.
"Who are you?" I asked. No answer. I closed my eyes
again. I felt her touch against my skin. She was
gentle and warm. My clothes melted from me as the
snow melts from earth on a warm early spring day. I
shivered as she kissed me. On the neck at first, and
then lower. Lower, oh so low. I felt warmer than I
ever felt before. I arched my back in ecstasy.
When her lips returned to mine, I felt whole as we
made love. When we were spent and we held each other
for what seemed hours, she lifted from me and in a wisp
she was gone.

"Who were you?" I asked. No answer.
I realized that the rain had stopped now. There was
silence. Silence and longing. Even though the urge
was gone, the desire lingered.
"Who was there?" I asked. No answer, or was there? I
thought I heard someone say, "goodbye Giovanni. Goodbye my
sweet Giovanni."
The wind was whispering in the trees.

Hand me your heart

If you hand me your heart when you feel it is time
I'll treasure the gift like fruit on the vine.
For what you have given I will carefully nourish
when the love has matured inside then I will cherish.
Gently press to my lips and carefully taste
every drop of love from within, not a drop to waste.
Warmth will glow in my cheeks and all through my soul.
You have fed my love for you, which will continue to grow.

*The author doing his Pee Wee Herman imitation
with his sisters at their home on Watson Ave.*

LaVergne, TN USA
03 February 2010

171997LV00003B/1/P